FROM WORST TO FIRST!

The Improbable 1991 Seasons of the Atlanta Braves and the Minnesota Twins

by Bill Gutman, Dave Weiner and Tony Seidl

TOR

A TOM DOHERTY ASSOCIATES BOOK
NEW YORK

FROM WORST TO FIRST!

Copyright © 1991 T. D. Media, Inc.

A Tor Book
Published by Tom Doherty Associates, Inc.
49 West 24th Street
New York, N.Y. 10010

Tor® is a registered trademark of Tom Doherty Associates, Inc.

Cover photos/insert photos provided by TV Sports Mailbag Inc./Photo File

ISBN: 0-812-52077-7

First edition: December 1991

Printed in the United States of America

0 9 8 7 6 5 4 3 2 1

Dedication

To Kathy —B.G.

To Charlene, my "guru" Ken Kaiman, my buddy Al Reed, Chris and Martha, and Bruce and Rolf —D.W.

To Sherry —T.S.

Introduction

A baseball first is always an event. Needless to say, there have been many such events in the long history of the game. Some firsts are in the form of records, which may subsequently be broken, then broken again. But others firsts can only happen once. If they happen again, well, it doesn't really matter because it has already been done.

Until 1991, there was a kind of first-in-waiting, something that had never once happened since the advent of the modern two-league structure in the early 1900s. In fact, it was something that even the experts weren't sure would ever happen. No team had ever gone from finishing dead last one year to winning a pennant or division title the next.

Before the establishment of divisional play in 1969, the team finishing first automatically won the pennant. But there were no worst-to-first finishes. After 1969, there were a pair of divisional winners in each league, giving each team twice the chances to make the ultimate leap. But not one ballclub could do it.

Worst to first. Think about it. If a team is so bad that it can't top any other ballclub in its division one year, how can it become so good that it tops every team the next? To go from worst to first, a ballclub has to have a number of things going for it. For starters, it helps if the last-place finish was something of a fluke. In other words, the team had more talent than it showed. Perhaps a combination of off seasons and injuries pulled the team down. A few key comebacks combined with a couple of shrewd trades or free-agent acquisitions, and the ballclub is right back in business. If a team is to go from worst to first, this is the scenario that will most likely make it possible.

But if a team finishes last because of a lack of talent—poor pitching, mediocre fielding, little power or clutch hitting, for example—then the rebuilding task is normally more than a one-year proposition. The quick fix generally does not work with a 25-man baseball team. In fact, some teams have tried to rebuild by spending millions upon millions of dollars on personnel, acquiring free agents and signing stars to multi-year contracts, and it hasn't worked. The teams are still mired among the mediocre.

Then came 1991. At the outset of the season,

the usual names were bandied about as potential divisional winners. There were the Blue Jays and Red Sox in the American League East; the powerful A's in the A.L. West. In the National League, talk of the Mets and Pirates dominated the East, while the defending champ Reds and resurgent Dodgers got most of the votes in the West. Any worst-to-first finishes were once again not even dreamed about.

That's what makes the 1991 season so special. There was finally a worst-to-first finish. But wait! There wasn't just one. There were two! Something that had never before happened in big-league baseball not only happened once in 1991, it happened twice. The Minnesota Twins in the American League West and the Atlanta Braves in the National League West were both divisional winners, both making that unheard-of jump from the bottom to the top.

The Twins had finished the 1990 season with a 74–88 record. To many, the outlook for '91 wasn't much better. But Manager Tom Kelly's ballclub surprised everyone with a 95–67 finish, winning by eight games in what may have been baseball's toughest division. En route to their unprecedented victory, the Twins also dethroned the three-time American League champion Oakland A's, considered one of the best teams of its era.

For the Braves, the victory may have been

even sweeter. A 65–97 finish in 1990 stamped the Atlanta ballclub as one of the worst in baseball. The Braves' long-suffering fans were beginning to stay away from the ballpark in droves. Then in '91 the club played well in the first half, staying in contention. For some fans, that was miracle enough. But when the Braves caught fire after the All-Star break and chased down the favored Dodgers, the whole city of Atlanta was gripped with championship fever. Manager Bobby Cox's team checked in with a division-winning 94–68 mark, topping the Dodgers by a single game.

How did these two very different ballclubs beat some very long odds to become champions? Each traveled a separate path to become the talk of its league. The Twins were an example of a team that probably shouldn't have finished in the cellar in 1990. The Braves, on the other hand, just didn't seem to have the talent to make much of a move.

From Worst to First! follows both the Twins and the Braves from start to finish in 1991, beginning with a brief history of both franchises, then describing the off-season moves that strengthened each team. From there, the story of the divisional races emerges, a month-by-month chronicle of how each team made baseball history, along with the players who made it possible.

FROM WORST TO FIRST!

Of course, every good story has to have a dynamite ending. This one certainly does, because it tracks each team through the divisional playoffs and right into the fateful meeting in the 1991 World Series. With two teams making baseball history in the same season, could it have ended any other way?

Chapter One

The Minnesota Twins: A Look Back

Long before the divisional race of 1991, the Minnesota Twins had another distinction. They were part of baseball's first expansion back in 1961. That year, the American League broke the longstanding tradition of eight teams in each league by adding two new franchises. One was the then Los Angeles (later California) Angels. The second newly created franchise set up shop in Washington, D.C., and was called the Senators.

This gets a bit tricky because baseball fans know there was a Washington Senators franchise in the American League since the league was born in 1901. It was not a successful franchise, and a saying sprang up in the nation's capital: "Washington—first in war, first in peace, last in the American League."

The Senators won pennants in 1924, 1925 and 1933 and their only world championship in 1924. The first two teams are remembered for the legendary pitcher Walter Johnson, still considered by many to be the greatest ever. But other than that trio of seasons long ago, the Senator teams were rarely distinguished. By the 1950s the team was struggling once more. Attendance was down and owner Calvin Griffith was losing money. He began looking for greener pastures, a place to take his team for a fresh start. When Griffith learned that the American League was planning to expand, he convinced league officials to allow him to move the club to Minneapolis, where the team was renamed the Twins, for the twin cities of Minneapolis and St. Paul. That opened up Washington for the expansion team.

In Minneapolis, the Twins began showing signs of life almost immediately. The club had a number of fine ballplayers in 1961 and seemed better than its 70–90 finish indicated. Among the '61 Twins were future Hall of Fame slugger Harmon Killebrew, power hitters Bob Allison and Jim Lemon, catcher Earl Battey and a scrappy second baseman named Billy Martin. Camilo Pascual led a weak pitching staff.

By 1965, however, the Twins were made of even sterner stuff and won the American League pennant with a 102–60 mark. This was an outstanding team. Despite missing a good part of the season with an injury, Killebrew hit 25 homers and drove home 75 runs. Young Tony

Oliva won the A.L. batting title with a .321 average, hit 16 homers and drove home 98 runs. Jimmie Hall, the center fielder, had 20 dingers and 86 ribbies, while Allison had 23 and 78. First sacker Don Mincher had 22 and 65, while shortstop Zoilo Versalles had 19 and 77, becoming the league's Most Valuable Player along the way. This was a hard-hitting bunch, all right.

The club also had a solid pitching staff. Righthander Jim Grant, known as "Mudcat," led the way with a 21–7 record. Southpaw Jim Kaat was 18–11, while Jim Perry checked in at 12–7 and the veteran Pascual 9–3. Al Worthington was the top reliever with a 9–3 record and 21 saves. Managed by Sam Mele, the Twins extended a tough L.A. Dodger team to seven games before being beaten in the World Series. Had it not been for the mound heroics of the great Dodger southpaw Sandy Koufax, the Twins undoubtedly would have been world champs.

Though the ballclub remained competitive for the next several years, it could not repeat. In '66 the Twins were second as Killebrew hit 39 homers and Kaat won 25 games. A year later they missed by a single game as Killebrew slammed 44 homers and newcomer Dean Chance won 20. A rookie second baseman named Rod Carew batted .292 in the first year of a Hall of Fame career.

Then in 1968, the team faded, winding up at 79–83. Age and injuries began taking their toll.

But with Billy Martin becoming manager in 1969, the Twins celebrated the first year of divisional play by winning the West at 97–65. Killebrew was sensational, leading the league with 49 homers and 140 RBI's. Carew took the batting title at .332, while Oliva had a .309, 24, 101 year despite bad knees that would eventually shorten his career. Jim Perry and Dave Boswell were both 20-game winners, but the ballclub was beaten in the playoffs by the powerful Baltimore Orioles.

The same thing happened in 1970. The Twins were 98–64 as Killebrew and Oliva led the offense and Jim Perry the pitching with 24 wins. But once again the Orioles were too strong in the playoffs and Minnesota was denied access to the World Series. A 74–86 finish in 1971 more or less ended the run that had started in 1965. Now the team had to be rebuilt.

Throughout the remainder of the 1970s, the franchise had competitive clubs, but not outstanding ones. However, by 1982 the Twins were at rock bottom, holding up the division with a 60–102 record. Yet there was already a small nucleus of players who would soon begin building something special all over again. First sacker Kent Hrbek, third baseman Gary Gaetti, right fielder Tom Brunansky, catcher Tim Laudner and a young left-hander named Frank Viola would all stick around as the team was slowly restructured.

The Twins were 70–92 the next year, then improved to 81–81 in 1984. Center fielder Kirby Puckett had joined the team by then, and a year later shortstop Greg Gagne and pitcher Bert Blyleven were aboard, though the team slid back to 77–85. Then came 1986, a strange year.

There was power to spare. Gaetti hit 34 homers and drove in 108 runs. Puckett had 31 and 96, while hitting .328. Short and compact, possessed of both power and speed, he had become a superstar. Hrbek blasted 29 and drove in 91, while Brunansky slammed 23 and designated hitter Roy Smalley had 20. Right-hander Blyleven led the pitchers with 17 wins, while Viola had 16. Yet the club lacked secondary pitching and finished at 71–91, just four games ahead of last-place Seattle, another expansion ballclub. The Twins also changed managers with just 23 games left in the season, Tom Kelly taking over for Ray Miller.

That's why no one was prepared for what happened in 1987. Playing in a division where teams seemed to look for ways not to win, the Twins suddenly found themselves in a pennant race. Had they not finished four games ahead of Seattle the year before, there would have been worst-to-first stories in 1987. The California Angels had won the A.L. West in '86 by five games over the Texas Rangers. They were the only two teams with better than .500 records.

In '87, both the Angels and Rangers crashed, finishing sixth and seventh, respectively, and opening the race up to the also-rans of a year earlier. The Kansas City Royals had good power and pitching, as well as a rookie named Bo Jackson. Oakland was an up-and-coming power-house, with youngsters Jose Canseco and Mark McGwire hitting 80 homers between them, and right-hander Dave Stewart winning 20 games. The A's were just a year away from a three-year dynasty.

As the days dwindled to a precious few, it was the Twins, Royals and A's in a dogfight for the title. Minneapolis finally won it with an 85–77 record, finishing two games ahead of the Royals and four in front of the A's. Once again the Twins did it mainly with their bats. Hrbek, Gaetti and Brunansky all had more than 30 homers, while Puckett had 28 and hit a team-leading .332. The pitching, however, appeared painfully thin. Only Viola (17–10) and Blyleven (15–12) won more than 10 games. Young Les Straker, at 8–10, was considered the number three starter. But Jeff Reardon was a premier closer with 31 saves, while setup man Juan Berenguer had an 8–1 mark with 4 saves. It was in the playoffs and World Series, however, that the Twins found they had an ally, almost a 26th man.

FROM WORST TO FIRST!

It was their home park, the Hubert H. Humphrey Metrodome. This strange stadium, nicknamed the Homerdome for the ease with which players could slam the ball into the seats, also had an extremely hard playing surface and a strange white roof that was held in place by air pressure. The stadium also had poor acoustics, and the noise generated by a full house of more than 50,000 screaming fans was nearly deafening.

In the playoffs, the Twins used their powerful bats to quiet the Detroit Tigers in five games, winning the first two at the Metrodome and then two of three at Tiger Stadium. But the pitching was still uncertain. Blyleven won two games with a 4.05 earned run average. Viola won one, but his ERA was 5.25. Reliever Reardon was at 5.06 and Straker was bombed to the tune of a 16.88 ERA. That's why the St. Louis Cardinals were made solid favorites in the World Series.

It turned into one of the strangest Series on record. In fact, it was the first seven-game Series ever in which the home team won every game. Fortunately for the Twins, four of the games were played at the Metrodome. A combination of the noise, the Twins' batting and some surprisingly fine pitching—especially by Frank Viola—did the trick. In fact, the boisterous fans, waving a sea of white "homer hankies," may have helped to unnerve the Cardinals.

Minneapolis won the first two at home, lost three straight at St. Louis, then came back to take the final pair and become champions. Viola gave up just one run in eight innings of the opener and two runs in eight innings of the seventh and final game to become the MVP.

The Twins' hitters batted .329 at home, while hitting just .184 at St. Louis. By contrast, the Cardinal pitchers had a 1.67 ERA at Busch Stadium, but in the Metrodome it ballooned to an overinflated 9.00. That's how effective the Twins were at home.

"I can't even begin to describe how far this organization has come," said right fielder Tom Brunansky. "We were bad. Worse than bad. And look what we are now. World champions!"

The team had an even better season in 1988, winning 91 games. But no one in the A.L. West could touch the emerging Oakland A's. Despite 24 wins from Viola and a .356, 24, 121 super year from Puckett, the ballclub finished 13 games behind the A's.

A year later, the team suddenly seemed to go into eclipse. It fell to fifth with an 80–82 mark, with some of the stars having off seasons. Viola nosedived to an 8–12 record after having won the Cy Young Award a year earlier. Puckett led the league with a .339 average, but hit just 9 homers and drove home only 85 runs, low for him. Others fell off slightly. Blyleven had moved on to California, but lefty Allan Anderson filled the void at 17–10. Reardon was still outstanding in the pen, but the second-line starters were weak and the club couldn't make up for Viola's slump.

Going into 1990, there were questions about which direction the club would take. If it continued to falter, wholesale changes might be in order. The fans couldn't forget the great championship season of 1987. They wanted more. The Twins had been a solid franchise since migrating from Washington to Minnesota. So there was certainly reason for optimism.

Chapter Two

The Atlanta Braves: A Look Back

They didn't always play in Atlanta. No, these Braves go back a long way, arriving in Atlanta at the end of a three-city odyssey that saw the franchise achieve measures of success at both previous stops. Before becoming the Atlanta Braves, the franchise was the Milwaukee Braves and before that the Boston Braves. All that adds up to the longest continuously active franchise in baseball history.

The Boston franchise became a charter member of the National Association, the first professional league, when it was formed in 1871. From 1872 to 1875 the team, called the Red Stockings, finished first each year. Then it joined the newly formed National League in 1876. Soon the team became known as the Beaneaters, winning eight pennants before the turn of the century.

At the beginning of the 20th century the ballclub changed its name to the Braves. In 1914, managed by George Stallings, the team became the talk of baseball by coming from last place with just two months left in the season to win the National League pennant with a 94–59 record. The Braves then upset the favored Philadelphia Athletics in the World Series, earning the nickname of the "Miracle Braves."

After that, however, the team fell on hard times. From 1917 through 1945, the ballclub finished over .500 just five times. In 1946, a contractor named Lou Perini bought the ballclub and set about rebuilding it. By 1948, there was another pennant winner, a solid team led by the righty-lefty pitching combo of Johnny Sain and the great Warren Spahn.

"Spahn and Sain, and pray for rain," was the chant heard around Braves Field, because the rest of the pitching staff wasn't very strong. But the hitters were. Five of the starters hit over .300, led by Tommy Holmes, Al Dark and Eddie Stanky. Bob Elliott was the top power hitter, with 23 homers and 100 RBI's. In the World Series that year, the Braves gave it a good try but lost to a fine Cleveland Indians team in six games.

A year later the team fell to 75–79, and attendance fell as well. By 1952 the ballclub was beset by woes on every front. The team had plummeted to seventh place at 64–89. Braves Field was an anachronism, and attendance was down 80 percent from the pennant-winning year of 1948. Owner Perini decided to make a radical change, a change that would start a new trend in baseball.

Before the 1953 season he decided to move the franchise to Milwaukee, the first franchise shift in the major leagues in 50 years. A year later, the St. Louis Browns would move to Baltimore, and four years after that the baseball world would be shocked when the Brooklyn Dodgers migrated west to Los Angeles and the New York Giants headed for San Francisco. The topographical face of baseball was forever changed.

But the Braves were the first and in Milwaukee the team became an overnight success. Not only did the ballclub set a new major-league attendance record with more than 1.8 million fans, but it surprised on the field as well by finishing second to the Dodgers with a 92–62 record. The team would remain powerful for the rest of the decade.

The club was building a nucleus of fine young players. In 1953 that group included Eddie Mathews, who led the league with 47 homers; Joe Adcock; Johnny Logan; Bill Bruton and Del Crandall. Spahn won 23 games and was joined by right-handers Lew Burdette and Bob Buhl to form a Big Three. A year later a rookie outfielder named Hank Aaron joined the team. He would become a legend.

17

By 1956 the club was getting closer, losing to Brooklyn by a single game. Then in 1957 the Braves broke through, winning the National League pennant with a 95–59 record. The acquisition of second sacker Red Schoendienst was the final link. Aaron was already a superstar, Mathews a super slugger, Spahn still a perennial 20-game winner. Both the bench and the bullpen were deep. In the World Series that year the Braves gave their fans the ultimate, defeating the mighty New York Yankees in seven games. Lew Burdette was the hero, winning three complete game victories, including the last two by shutout. Aaron was the league's Most Valuable Player.

The team proved that that had been no fluke the next year, winning a second straight pennant with the same great cast of characters. This time the Yanks won the Series in seven, but the Braves were surely among baseball's best. In '59, the club lost to the Dodgers in a playoff for the pennant. Aaron won the batting title at .355, adding 39 homers and 123 RBI's. Mathews was the league's homer champ with 46, hitting .306 and driving home 114 runs. Spahn and Burdette won 21 each. A great ballclub.

There was another second-place finish in 1960 before the ballclub began to fade. By 1962 the Braves were fifth at 86–76 as the National League expanded to 10 teams. A couple more of those mediocre finishes and the honeymoon was over in Milwaukee. The fans began staying away in the same droves that had surged through the turnstiles in the early years.

The 1965 team continued to post a winning record but finished fifth again. With attendance continuing to dwindle, the club decided to move once more. This time the Braves headed south, in 1966 emerging as the Atlanta Braves. Playing in a new stadium that was affectionately dubbed "the launching pad," the Braves had a heavy-hitting ballclub that year, good enough to finish at 85–77 in fifth place. It was typical of the team's efforts throughout the 1960s.

Aaron was still great, leading the league with 44 homers and 127 RBI's. Filipe Alou, Rico Carty and Joe Torre all hit over .300, Torre also blasting 36 homers and driving home 101 runs. Alou hit 31, Mack Jones 23 and the fading Mathews 16. What the team needed to contend, however, was more pitching.

It didn't happen until 1969. That was the first year of divisional play in the big leagues, and the Braves became the first National League West champion, finishing at 93–69. The hitting stars were Aaron, Orlando Cepeda, Clete Boyer, Felix Millan, Tony Gonzalez and Carty. The club also had a strong bench. Knuckleballer Phil Niekro won 23 games, with starting help from Ron Reed (18–10), Pat Jarvis and George Stone.

Cecil Upshaw anchored the bullpen.

With the advent of divisional play came a best-of-five playoff series to determine the pennant winners. Atlanta had to play the New York Mets, a so-called miracle team that had caught the proverbial lightning in a bottle and come from ninth the year before all the way to first in the N.L. East. Bolstered by an outstanding pitching staff, the Mets promptly eliminated the Braves in three straight games.

After that, the team's fortunes began to fade. It was fifth at 76–88 in 1970. Aaron had 47 homers and 118 RBI's in 1971, but there weren't too many other bright spots. Hammerin' Hank was on his way to becoming baseball's all-time home run leader. But he would break Babe Ruth's record with a struggling team. There was a bit of a revival (88–74) when Aaron finally hit his 715th in 1974, but a 67–94 mark the next year reflected the lack of talent on the team. A year after that, in 1976, it was in last place.

The team was really hurting, as demonstrated by 101 losses in 1977 and four different managers during the year, including a one-game stint in the dugout by new owner Ted Turner, who was subsequently told by the Commissioner of Baseball that owners couldn't manage. Bobby Cox was the new manager in 1978, but the team still finished last. Same thing in '79. Cox took over a very bad ballclub, but his efforts and baseball acumen wouldn't be forgotten.

There was a revival in 1982 under former star Joe Torre. The Braves surprised everyone that year by winning the N.L. West with an 89–73 record. Dale Murphy was the team's new standout, whacking 36 homers and driving home a league-best 109 runs in an MVP year. Bob Horner cracked 32 homers, while vet Chris Chambliss hit 20. Niekro at 17–4 was still the mound mainstay, but the rest of the staff was mediocre. In the playoffs, the club lost to the St. Louis Cardinals in three straight. Still no pennant for the fans of Atlanta.

By 1985 the club was near the bottom again at 66–96. A year later, under veteran skipper Chuck Tanner, it was last once more. One change, however, was the return of Bobby Cox as general manager. Cox had left in 1982 to manage the Toronto Blue Jays and had taken an American League East title with the Jays in '85. Now he had to try to rebuild the Braves.

The club moved up one notch in '87, finishing at 69–92. Murphy was still good enough to hit 44 homers and drive home 105. But the rest of the personnel were unstable. The lack of solid talent was everywhere. It was difficult to visualize the Braves making any kind of move in the near future. When the club checked in with a last-place, 54–106, record in 1988, it seemed that things couldn't get much worse. Manager

Tanner was replaced by Russ Nixon, but that didn't help. There was still another cellar finish in 1989.

But maybe there was a ray of hope. A pair of young pitchers, right-hander John Smoltz and southpaw Tom Glavine, had winning records. Yet another young prospect, outfielder Ron Gant, hit just .177 in 260 at bats. Would the futility ever end? It was becoming increasingly obvious that the club needed major changes, a real overhaul. It had been in last place three of the past four seasons. The fans were getting restless and attendance was down. It almost seemed like *déjà vu* from both the Boston and the Milwaukee days. In addition, there were complaints about the ballpark, the attitude of the fans and even the condition of the field.

Something had to be done . . . and fast.

Chapter Three

The 1990 Season—
What Does It Mean?

The 1990 season didn't begin well for anyone. It was the year of the lockout, the owners refusing to open training camps to the players because of stalemated contract negotiations between the Players Association and management. A shortened spring training could only hurt teams like the Twins and Braves, which needed the time to evaluate any young talent who might help.

Minnesota had already made a major move during the second half of the '89 season. It shipped its ace hurler, Frank Viola, to the New York Mets for a trio of young arms. At the time of the trade, Viola was struggling at 8–12. Coming to the Twins were right-handers Rick Aguilera and Kevin Tapani, as well as lefty David West. Only Aguilera was a proven quantity, but he had battled arm problems and had been used as both a starter and a reliever. At first, it seemed like a questionable trade for the Twins.

Even before the lockout ended, the early prognostications didn't make either team look good. A *Sporting News* columnist picked the Braves for last once more in the N.L. West. The analysis mentioned the young pitchers—Smoltz, Glavine, Derek Lilliquist and Pete Smith—adding, "Their day will come, but not yet." It also mentioned as a positive the acquisition of veteran left-hander Charlie Liebrandt and the elevation of rookie southpaw Mike Stanton.

The team also signed free agent Nick Esasky, who was coming off a career year in Boston, as well as power hitter Jim Presley. If those two newcomers worked out, the Braves would be adding power at both infield corners, first and third.

As for the Twins, the *Sporting News* analysis had them finishing sixth in the A.L. West, topping only the Chicago White Sox. Once more it was acknowledged that the ballclub had solid hitting with Puckett, Hrbek and Gaetti. But there was a catch. "The Twins pitching, with Allan Anderson as the ace, is suspect. If the young pitchers develop rapidly, the Twins could do as high as fourth."

The preseason proved little. The Twins were 6–9. They picked up veteran backup catcher Junior Ortiz to replace vet Tim Laudner, who left the team unexpectedly. Everyone knew the ballclub had hitting. An awful lot seemed to depend on the young pitchers—Tapani, West, Mark Guthrie and Mike Dyer: But as one article said: "The four haven't made anyone forget Frank Viola yet."

As for the Braves, they checked in with a surprising 7–7 in the preseason. Perhaps the toughest decision the team had to make in the spring was to release veteran slugger Darrell Evans, who would end a 19-year career with 414 home runs.

"It wasn't a fun day for me," said Braves manager Russ Nixon. "This is the worst day for managers. You have kids, and they know they're going down, but then you have guys like Darrell. You walk off the field not knowing if you're ever putting the uniform on again. That's a tough feeling."

But when the season opened, Nixon was optimistic. "What a difference," he said, referring to his team. "It could be a very good club and I feel this year we'll be in the middle of things. Once that happens, then anything can happen. This is the best club I've ever had to manage. It was tough coming to the ballpark last year, but this year I look forward to it."

Nixon added that he was looking for a .500 season from his team. That would represent a big improvement over the season before, when the club had finished 34 games under .500 and 28 games out of first. The team also brought up a young catcher from Richmond named Greg Olson. Like the young pitchers, he too had previously been in the Mets organization.

The Twins opened the 1990 season with a lineup that saw Dan Gladden in left, Randy Bush in right, Puckett in center, Hrbek at first, Gaetti at third, Brian Harper catching, Gene Larkin as the designated hitter, Gagne at short and Al Newman at second. Anderson was on the hill, and the team lost to defending champion Oakland.

For the Braves it was newcomer Oddibe McDowell in center, Jeff Treadway at second, Tommy Gregg in left, Esasky at first, Murphy in right, veteran Ernie Whitt catching, Presley at third, Jeff Blauser at short and Tom Glavine pitching. The Braves lost to the San Francisco Giants. Of the two basic lineups, the Twins seemed the more solid team.

It didn't take long for the writing to appear on the wall, especially for the Braves. After 10 games Atlanta was back in the basement at 2–8, already 7 games behind hot-starting Cincinnati and with the worst record in the league. Minnesota was in the middle of the pack at 6–7, just 3½ behind defending champ Oakland.

The Twins made one early-season move, naming Rick Aguilera, their bullpen stopper, the closer. It was a role vacated by Jeff Reardon, who had left via free agency after 1989. The Braves were already worried about John Smoltz, who had been an All-Star as a rookie the year before. He was rocked in his first two outings, and the bullpen had been awful. Manager Nixon sounded like a guy already feeling the heat.

"I take everything personally," he said. "I'm not putting the blame on anybody but myself. You always feel there's something more you should do. I carry a pretty heavy load home with me."

Such is the life of a last-place manager. And there's another problem with managing a perennially last-place team. It's called job security. By the All-Star break Nixon was gone, replaced by General Manager Bobby Cox, who would wear two hats for the remainder of the season.

"The first half just didn't go right," Cox said. "We came out of the box rough and it just got worse with injuries. We just couldn't get on track. It's been a little disappointing. We could be in second place if we had just played a little bit."

It wasn't easy visualizing the Braves in second place. The midyear report card for the team just wasn't good. Shortly after the All-Star break, the team had a 34–50 record, 19 games behind Cincinnati and just a half game ahead of Houston.

FROM WORST TO FIRST!

Though the team was still struggling, there had been some pleasant surprises, as well as a few disappointments.

For openers, longtime star Dale Murphy wasn't having a good year. Through July 8, Murph was hitting just .226, though he still led the club in RBI's with 43. Another big disappointment was the strange problem that scuttled the season of free agent Nick Esasky. Esasky was suffering from vertigo, a dizziness that wouldn't go away. The doctors seemed puzzled about the cause, and his year ended after just nine games.

Two pleasant surprises were Ron Gant and rookie David Justice. Gant had a sub-.200 batting average a year earlier, but as of July 8 was hitting a solid .318 with a team-best 17 homers and 40 RBI's. He also had 10 stolen bases and was looking like a possible coming star. So was Justice. A rookie first sacker who came up after the start of the season, the southpaw swinger was starting to show some power with 5 homers and 20 ribbies.

Second sacker Treadway was hitting .297 and catcher Olson .289. Olson was another pleasant surprise, since the veteran Whitt was nowhere at .169. Presley was a solid .270 with 11 homers and 42 RBI's. Shortstop Jeff Blauser was also solid at .286. But the bench was weak and as a team the Braves were hitting just .248, third worst in the league.

From Worst to First!

The pitching was also something of a disappointment. Smoltz and Glavine, the two youngsters, were both at .500 with records of 6–6 and 5–5, respectively. Pete Smith was at 5–6, while vet Charlie Liebrandt, coming off an injury, was 3–1. After the season began the team brought up a 20-year-old left-hander named Steve Avery. Avery was tagged a coming star by most experts, but it was apparent he needed seasoning. After five starts he was 1–3 with a 4.23 ERA. In fact, the staff ERA of 5.03 was by far the poorest in the league. So pitching was really the biggest problem as the second half of the season began.

The Twins were still fighting for respectability. Shortly after the All-Star break the Minnesotans had a 42–46 record, 13½ games behind Oakland. But only the surprising White Sox were chasing the A's. Everyone else was in a tight pack. The Twins were just two and a half games from third place, and only four and a half games separated the last five teams in the division.

As expected, the ballclub was hitting. Its .267 team batting average was second in the entire league, but the pitching was close to the bottom. Puckett was having another fine year at the plate, as were catcher Harper, Dan Gladden, Shane Mack and Hrbek. The club was scoring runs. As for the Braves, pitching seemed to be the Twins' biggest problem.

FROM WORST TO FIRST!

Allan Anderson, the top winner in '89, had nosedived to a 2–11 mark. His future was suddenly questionable. Kevin Tapani was the top winner at 9–5; Rick Aguilera had saved 21 games and Dave West was 4–7. So pitchers who had come from the Mets in the Viola deal were looking good. Veteran Juan Berenguer was 6–1 out of the bullpen and another vet, John Candelaria, had a 7–3 mark, mainly out of the pen. But for relievers to have that kind of record the starters had to be struggling.

There was little doubt that this ballclub had promise. In fact, the team was one of the hottest in the big leagues in May, compiling a 21–7 record for the month. But in June it reversed, going 7–21. The starters had a combined 21–36 mark and 4.95 ERA with just four complete games. The bullpen, on the other hand, was 19–7 with a 3.25 ERA.

"You'd like to see guys pick each other up better than we have," said Manager Kelly. "When Hrbek went into a slump in June, instead of guys rallying around him, they went into the tank with him. If a pitcher makes a bad pitch, the boys will rally around him and pick him up. The pitcher has to do the same thing when a fielder makes an error. We also have to do better at shutting down the other team when we do score. Too many times, we've gotten some runs on the board and then gone out and given it up."

FROM WORST TO FIRST!

The second half of the season went about the same for the Twins, but got even worse for the Braves. With the pitching continuing to struggle, the Twins wound up with a 74–87 record, last by a game and a half. Yet in a strange division, the team was just nine games out of third. But that didn't make the trip to the cellar any easier.

"We're in a rebuilding program and we'll have to suffer through it," said veteran sacker Kent Hrbek. "Hopefully, we'll develop the young pitchers before we [the veterans] start losing it."

It wasn't an overly optimistic outlook. Even the hitting had collapsed in the final month. Over the season, the ballclub lost 17 games in which it held the opponent to two runs or less. The club had more errors (101) than home runs (100), and the home run total was the lowest since 1980. In addition, the team hit just 57 homers after May 28 and only 46 at the Metrodome for the season. That was a record low.

Puckett, the team's best all-around hitter, slumped to .298, his first sub-.300 season since 1985, and he didn't hit a home run after July 15, finishing with just 12 for the season. Hrbek had 22 homers, but spent the last 10 days of the season watching after he sprained an ankle horsing around with the clubhouse attendants in the locker room. It was that kind of year.

The leading hitter was outfielder Shane Mack, who batted .326 in 313 at bats. He could be a coming star. Catcher Harper had a .294 season, while Hrbek batted .287 and Dan Gladden .275. But longtime slugger Gary Gaetti slumped to just .229 with 16 homers. Although the team was tied for fourth in the league in hitting at .265, only two teams scored fewer runs.

As for the pitching, that was also a cause for concern. Tapani was the top winner at 12–8. No other hurler won as many as 10 games. Anderson was an awful 7–18. Pete Smith was 5–10, David West 7–9. Aguilera made the conversion to closer with 32 saves, while Berenguer was a great setup man at 8–5. One bright spot was a young right-hander named Scott Erickson, who came up during the second half of the year and compiled an 8–4 record with a 2.87 ERA in 19 games.

At the end of 1990 it appeared that the Twins needed change. They might not be a bona fide last-place team. If a couple of the young pitchers matured and the hitters rebounded, they might get back to the middle of the pack or even to third. To go beyond that, they needed help.

The Braves were another story. They finished the season last again, and at 65–97 with the worst record in the major leagues. Not only did they have the worst mark in 1990, but they were the worst in baseball since 1985, compiling a 387–576 record during that time. As the headline in one paper read, "Bad management, bad deals, bad luck stagger franchise."

Everyone seemed to agree that the team just hadn't been able to settle on a solid rebuilding plan.

"This organization has flip-flopped so many times about what it wants to do," said former Braves star Hank Aaron, who was a senior vice-president with the team. "One year they decide to work through the free-agent market, the next year they go with young kids. You've got to have a plan and stay with it."

Bad trades and bad luck seemed to be dogging the franchise, all right. In 1985 the ballclub gave relief superstar Bruce Sutter a six-year, $10-million contract. Shoulder problems ended Sutter's career only 40 saves later. Even the signing of Nick Esasky before 1990 seemed to backfire. Esasky was paid $5.6 million for three years, but the vertigo that limited him to nine games in 1990 was still with him.

As the Braves floundered in the second half, they decided to make a major trade. Longtime star Dale Murphy was sent to the Philadelphia Phillies in August. In return, the Braves got pitcher Jeff Parrett, outfielder Jim Vatcher and shortstop Victor Rosario. None would become a household name. Yet just two years earlier, the Mets had offered a package of Howard Johnson, Lenny Dykstra and others for Murphy and the

Braves had turned it down.

General Manager Cox threw the criticism aside. "It doesn't bother me a bit," he said. "People can write or say what they want. We've stuck to our plan to try to build the organization and make it stronger. We feel we have direction. We have a lot of young guys here and we're hanging onto them. I think it's going to pay off."

In 1990, the team had the third worst batting average in the league, but there were bright spots. Veteran Lonnie Smith hit .305, though he was somewhat of a liability in the field. Gant continued his fine play and finished at .303 with 32 homers, 84 RBI's and 33 stolen bases. Justice came on like gangbusters and hit .282 with 28 homers and 78 ribbies. He was a cinch for Rookie of the Year honors. Catcher Olson had a solid .262 season and was outstanding behind the plate. He also made the All-Star team. Though third sacker Presley hit 19 homers, he was a free agent and talked about leaving. Young players like Jeff Treadway, Jeff Blauser and Mark Lemke were still unknown quantities. There was a nucleus, but it was a small one.

Same with the pitching. Smoltz finished at 14–11, Glavine at 10–12. The veteran Leibrandt was 9–11, while young Steve Avery struggled to finish at 3–11 with a 5.64 ERA. He might need more seasoning. But the team didn't have a reliable closer or much secondary pitching. It was last in the league in team ERA and in saves.

Unlike the Twins, whom many considered somewhat better than their last-place finish, the Braves were considered a bona fide last-place team, a ballclub that was still going to have difficulty rising even a notch or two in the standings in 1991. For that rise to happen, a lot of young players would have to mature in a hurry. And the team would have to make some major deals or sign some outstanding free agents. At the end of 1990 any of that seemed unlikely.

But there was a lot of impatience in Atlanta. Unlike Minnesota, where the fans had cheered a world champion as recently as 1987, the Braves had been struggling for years. In fact, since divisional play had begun in 1969, the Braves had been last or next to last 13 times in 21 years. One person who was getting impatient was team president Stan Kasten.

"When I got here five years ago, this team was aging and overpaid," he said. "At least we've turned that around. Now, this is a young team with bright prospects and I think we're closer to improving than we were five years ago. I think we all know we have to turn this around. We're all tired of waiting."

There wouldn't be much more time for talking

FROM WORST TO FIRST!

in either Minneapolis or Atlanta. With the extended baseball season there was precious little room for off-season activity. In other words, 1991 was just around the corner.

Chapter Four

Getting Ready for 1991

Most baseball teams don't stand pat anymore, not even the good ones. A good team that wants to keep most or all of its players may simply find some of their contract demands too steep. Players who qualify for free agency sometimes decide to move on even though they're playing with a winner. But in the winter of 1990–91, it was apparent that both the Braves and the Twins would have to make some moves.

Atlanta moved first. In October, shortly after the end of the World Series of 1990, the ballclub announced a major front-office move. John Schuerholz, who had been a highly successful general manager at Kansas City, was hired to fill the same post with the Braves. That would free up Bobby Cox to concentrate on his job as field manager. Cox had been GM since 1985, and some wondered whether the two men would get along.

"From my perspective, there's no problem,"

said Schuerholz. "I'm delighted that Bobby knows how difficult it is to put a team together, and equally delighted in his desire to want to manage again."

As for Cox, he was also ready for a singular role. "I don't look at [managing] as pressure," he said. "I'm just going to work as hard as I can and do the best job I can and let the chips fall."

Schuerholz also vowed to "make the Braves a championship organization," and in the ensuing months he started to do just that. If it meant spending owner Ted Turner's money, Schuerholz—with Turner's blessing—was prepared to do that. The free-agent market can be a tricky proposition. Some free agents have produced magnificently. Others have simply flopped. And in either case, it costs the signing team millions of dollars. The Braves didn't plunge into the free-agent market with reckless abandon. They signed a number of players, however, all calculated to improve the team. But that's everyone's goal. As with all signings, there was some element of risk.

With Jim Presley leaving, the club needed a third baseman. The best one available was Terry Pendleton, a 30-year-old switch hitter who had been with the Cardinals since 1984. An outstanding fielder and line-drive hitter, Pendleton had a high of 96 RBI's with the Cards in 1987, but had never hit more than 13 home runs. He was also coming off a horrible 1990 season in which he had hit a career-low .230. Injuries had limited him to just 121 games and he had just 6 homers and 58 RBI's.

Was it just an off year or was Pendleton starting on the downside? Rumor had it that the Yankees also wanted the former Card, but Pendleton opted to stay in the National League and signed with the Braves. He was considered a good pickup.

The next two moves were looked upon as questionable. The Braves signed first sacker Sid Bream, who had been the Pirates' regular first baseman since 1986. Bream was also 30, had some power, but also had bad knees. He had been limited to 19 games by injury in 1989, but had bounced back to have a solid .270 season in 1990, adding 15 homers and 67 ribbies in 147 games. With Bream in the lineup, the Braves could move young David Justice to the outfield, where they believed he would be more comfortable.

The club also signed veteran catcher Mike Heath, a 36-year-old who had hit .270 with Detroit in 1990. Heath was considered a scrapper and leader, a good complement to Olson behind the plate. Also coming on board was pitcher Juan Berenguer, also 36, who had been with the Twins since 1987 and in the big leagues since 1978. The Braves saw Berenguer as a veteran reliever who could still throw hard and might fill the role of closer if no one else stepped into it.

Another minor acquisition was 29-year-old shortstop Rafael Belliard. Belliard had been strictly a utility player with the Pirates since 1982, playing more than 100 games only twice. He had hit just .204 in 1990 and was penciled in as the third shortstop behind Andres Thomas and Blauser. Many thought he wouldn't even make the team.

Then there was another signing that made big news even if it didn't have a projected big impact. The ballclub signed outfielder Deion Sanders, who had played part of the 1990 season with the Yankees, hitting just .158. "Neon Deion," or "Prime Time," as he liked to be called, was a two-sport performer, an outstanding cornerback with the Atlanta Falcons of the NFL who also wanted to play baseball.

Unlike Bo Jackson, who played the entire baseball season, then left to play football (before his injury), Sanders had a contract which called for him to leave his baseball team in July so that he could play the entire football season. Sanders still hadn't proved he could hit major-league pitching with regularity, but because he played football in Atlanta, the Braves thought it was a natural to give him a shot.

"You need to get a little more hyped up to

play football," Sanders said. "Defensive backs are probably the cockiest men on the field because they have to be. They're being challenged on every play. It's just a mentality. But you don't have to be two different people [to play football and baseball]; you just have to know how to adjust."

So there were some interesting additions. With the exception of Berenguer, however, the Braves didn't tamper with their pitching staff. General Manager Schuerholz and Manager Cox decided to go with the three youngsters— Smoltz, Glavine and Avery—and the veteran Leibrandt. A fifth starter would come from the other arms in camp. As spring training approached, the Braves believed they had definitely strengthened their team.

The Twins, also, had no plans to make wholesale changes. They believed their veteran hitters still gave them a solid core and that the young arms would come around. They did want to obtain one good veteran pitcher, maybe a number one, but that wouldn't be easy. They also found themselves with a need for a third baseman after veteran Gary Gaetti announced he was planning to leave the team via free agency.

When they signed a pitcher the news was greeted with some skepticism. Yes, Jack Morris was a big name, the winningest pitcher in the majors during the 1980s. But the right-hander, who had spent his entire career with the Detroit Tigers, would be 36 years old when the 1991 season began and was coming off two below-par seasons.

A two-time, 20-game winner, Morris was just 6–14 in 1989 and 15–18 in 1990. His ERA of 4.51 in 1990 wasn't good, but his arm was still sound, as proved by his 250 innings pitched and 11 complete games. The question was, could Morris regain his winning ways? He certainly would exert a positive influence on the younger pitchers. Maybe problem number one was solved.

The third base problem wasn't as easy. When the Twins signed free agent Mike Pagliarulo, many thought it was a mistake. Pags had once been a promising power hitter with the New York Yankees, belting a high of 32 dingers in 1987. But he inexplicably began losing his batting eye the next year, hitting just .216. After 74 games in 1989, he was shipped to San Diego and finished up a .197 hitter for the year with just seven homers. He bounced back to hit .254 with the Padres in 1990, but hit only seven more homers. Though he was still a fine fielder, most considered him finished as a hitter. Signing him was a gamble.

Another signing involved Chili Davis, a switch hitter who was with the California An-

gels in 1990. Davis had good power, hitting between 21 and 29 homers from 1982 to 1989. In
'90, he fell off to 12 homers and 58 RBI's. The
Twins wanted him as a designated hitter.

Also joining the team was veteran right-
hander Steve Bedrosian, who had been a fine
closer with the Phillies and Giants. "Bedrock,"
as he was called, had a league-best 40 saves in
1987, winning the Cy Young Award in the process. In 1990, he was still good enough to appear
in 68 games for the Giants, compiling a 9–9 record with 17 saves.

As the Twins got ready for 1991, Manager
Kelly and his staff believed their team was also
improved. If they got the hitting they expected
and if Morris regained his form and if the young
pitchers matured on schedule ... well, who
knows in baseball?

Despite the moves made by both the Braves
and the Twins, the so-called experts apparently
weren't convinced. Preseason prognostications
had both ballclubs sitting close to where they
had been the year before.

The Sporting News took a poll of more than
180 members of the Baseball Writers' Association of America. The picks were Oakland and
Toronto in the American League, the Dodgers
and Cubs in the National. Where were the Twins
and Braves? The writers had the Twins dead last

in the A.L. West, the only team in the American League that didn't get a single first-place vote. The Braves were picked for fifth in the N.L. West, with only the Houston Astros below them. Like the Twins, the Braves didn't get a single first-place vote.

A similar poll was conducted by *Sports Illustrated* magazine. This one picked California and Boston in the American League, the Cubs and Reds in the National. Once again the Twins and Braves were among the also-rans, Minneapolis picked for dead last and Atlanta a surprising fourth.

Though the Twins were playing surprisingly good ball during spring training, the writer of the analysis didn't think they could do that once the season began.

"The poor Twins," the article read, "they will play their tails off and finish last. But in the process, they will continue their well-planned rebuilding program."

Manager Kelly believed the hitters held the key to the season. They couldn't afford to go south, even if the pitching faltered. "When you're constantly down 3–0 and 4–0 in the fourth inning," he said, "hitters lose interest. That's what happened to us last year."

Though the analysis ended by saying, "The Twins can climb out of the toilet, but they won't get out of the cellar," Kelly saw things differently.

"We're going to surprise some people," he said. "We've got some starting pitching. I've never had that before."

The *Sports Illustrated* report on the Braves was slightly more optimistic. It quoted General Manager Bob Quinn of Cincinnati as saying, "We all see what the Dodgers and Giants have done. But the Braves—look at Pendleton and Bream and Heath. And they have a great outfield, as well."

Al Rosen, who ran the Giants, also believed the Braves might surprise. "They can't be overlooked," he said. "I've always thought Bobby Cox was an excellent manager, and he's got impact players in Gant and Justice."

But in the final analysis, it was thought the Braves just didn't have enough firepower to make a real impact in a tough division. And as the season finally approached, only time would tell.

Chapter Five

Getting Out of the Gate

Both the final week of spring training and the first week of the regular season are always important. Rosters have to be firmed up, last-minute moves made, starting lineups announced, and then every team has to try to get out of the gate fast. A fast start not only gives a team confidence, but also gets it in the thick of things in a hurry. This is especially important for teams such as the Twins and Braves, who did so poorly the season before. Add a horrendous start, and a losing attitude can creep into the clubhouse quickly.

Much of the early baseball news focused on the superstars. How would Darryl Strawberry fare now that he had left the Mets and signed with the Dodgers? Could Orel Hershiser come back from rotator cuff surgery? What about Bo Jackson? Would the serious hip injury he had suffered at the end of the previous football season end his athletic career in both sports? Minor transactions were relegated to the small print and the back page—except in the cities where they occurred.

The Braves

The Braves had released outfielder Oddibe McDowell, and also placed on the disabled list outfielder Lonnie Smith (who had undergone arthroscopic knee surgery) and first sacker Nick Esasky. The Esasky move was especially disturbing. The club had paid a lot of money to sign him before 1990. His mysterious vertigo still prevented him from playing. Smith was an aging player, but still a dangerous hitter in certain situations.

With Smith on the DL and the subsequent release of McDowell, the Braves were apparently turning over the left field job to Deion Sanders, a move that surprised a lot of people. But Sanders had played well in the spring, hustling and working hard to earn a job. He didn't come in with the attitude that he was a special case. He was just another young player battling for a position.

A week later, the ballclub acquired speedy

outfielder Otis Nixon from Montreal. Nixon had swiped 50 bases while playing in just 111 games for the Expos in 1990. The Braves also placed pitcher Pete Smith on the DL and released shortstop Andres Thomas, who had been with the club since 1985. Manager Cox then announced that Rafael Belliard would be the starting shortstop. That was another surprise move, since Belliard had been nothing more than a utility man during his days with the Pirates.

Also on the positive side, both John Smoltz and Steve Avery were looking very good in the spring. Avery, of course, was a disappointing 3–11 as a 20-year-old rookie in 1990. But now one report called the two "the best young 1–2 pitching punch in the N.L.," adding, "They are the keys to Atlanta's improvement."

Unfortunately, the Braves didn't start the season in red-hot fashion. They expected a sellout crowd of more than 52,000 at Atlanta-Fulton County Stadium for the opener, but were rained out for the second straight year. Their next two games combined drew 33,199 fans. Unless the team started playing well, attendance might indeed be down once more.

The ballclub opened up with Bream at first, Jeff Treadway and Mark Lemke sharing second, Belliard at short and Pendleton at third. The outfield consisted of Sanders and Nixon in left, Gant in center and Justice in right. Heath seemed to have the inside track to do the brunt of the catching, with Greg Olson as the backup. Manager Cox preferred four-man rotation in the early going, with Leibrandt and the three youngsters—Glavine, Avery and Smoltz. There was still no bona fide closer, unless the veteran Berenguer filled that role.

Things could have been worse the first week. The team split its first four games, Glavine and Avery winning, Leibrandt and Smoltz losing. Avery's victory over the defending champion Reds, 7–5, gave the team a lift, but Smoltz had given up four runs in just four and a third innings in his first start.

Also on the plus side were a couple of pinch hits by Tommy Gregg, a 3-for-4 performance by Olson in his only start, Lemke and Treadway both hitting well, and Justice leading the team with 5 RBI's. Gant, Sanders, Pendleton and Heath hadn't hit much the first week. That part didn't get much better the second week as the club fell into familiar territory—the basement. They had a 4–6 record and were just two and a half games off the pace, so it really wasn't much to worry about.

The only early-season concern was the lack of hitting with a few key players. Gant was off to a 4-for-37 start, and some remembered his sub-.200 season in 1989. Bream was hitting just .188 and Justice .211. On the plus side, the catching tandem of Heath and Olson was batting .333, but it was too early to pick up any kind of pattern. Perhaps the biggest surprise was the play of Deion Sanders, who was hitting just .226 but with a .333 on-base percentage. His bosses were impressed.

"He's been as good a player as we've put out there every night," said General Manager John Schuerholz. "He's played with fire, with aggressiveness, and he's been getting on base. He takes a pitch like a five-year veteran and he's worked his tail off this spring to make this team. We couldn't have asked any more of him."

During the next few weeks something was becoming very obvious to the opponents of the Braves. This was not the same walkover team they had been facing for the past five years. The young players and strong arms were beginning to make their presence felt.

"We've shown so far that teams aren't just going to come out and throw their jocks on the field and win two out of three against us," said utility infielder Jeff Blauser. "I think in the past teams have come in and taken us lightly, and we're doing our damnedest to change that."

They certainly were. The ballclub won six of its first eight road games, including a pair in Houston, where they'd been beaten nine straight the year before. A 2–1 victory in 13 innings in the Astrodome gave the club an 8–7 record, the first time they had been above the .500 mark since April 23, 1989. There would be a whole slew of "firsts" before the season ended.

By the end of the first month the club was hanging in at 11–11, tied for second with Los Angeles and just one and a half games behind co-leaders Cincinnati and San Diego. The only two areas of concern were the continued slump of center fielder Gant, who was hitting only .153 after an 0-for-12 week, and the continued struggling of Smoltz, who was 1–3. Otherwise, the team was playing well.

"I think the biggest change has been the play of our infield," said catcher Greg Olson. "They make the pitcher's job so much easier. Now our pitchers don't go out there scared anymore. They go out there and throw strikes."

The team was also getting outstanding play from Otis Nixon, who hit .364 in his first eight starts and already had 11 stolen bases. He was beginning to take playing time away from Sanders. If Sanders couldn't play every day, the club might decide to send him to Richmond. "He needs to be playing," said Manager Cox.

Then, during the fifth week of the season, the Braves made national headlines. The reason was simple. The team was playing so well that it moved into first place in the N.L. West. At the end of the week the club had a 15–12 record, giving it a one-game lead over both Cincinnati and Los Angeles. It was the first time a Braves team had tasted first place since June 8, 1984. Some people were beginning to look at it as more than just a fluke.

Pirate star Bobby Bonilla was impressed after Atlanta took two of three from the Bucs. Said Bonilla of the Braves, "They may be a player away from winning the division. You can see the sparkle in their eyes. They're hungry and tired of losing."

That part was true. But a division title? No team in the history of baseball had ever gone from last to first. It's probably safe to say the team still wasn't thinking championship. But there were plenty of reasons for its resurgence.

Shortstop Belliard, always a light hitter, drove in a career-high five runs in a game with St. Louis, then had three more the next night. The eight ribbies in two games gave him two more than his entire 1990 total with Pittsburgh. Right fielder Justice had at least one RBI in seven straight games, one short of the club record. Reliever Kent Mercker had given up just two hits and no runs in 12⅔ innings, while southpaw Mike Stanton, coming off a shoulder surgery in 1990, didn't allow an earned run in his first 12 games.

Both Tom Glavine and young Steve Avery were starting to dominate on the mound. Glavine was 4–2 with a 2.29 ERA, while Avery was at 4–1 with a 2.79. Leibrandt was 3–3, while Smoltz continued to struggle at 1–4. Mercker and Berenguer had three saves each out of the pen.

A week later the Dodgers had moved into first with a 20–15 record. But the Braves were hanging tough. They were now 18–14, just a half game back. San Diego and Cincinnati each trailed by three, while the Astros and Giants were struggling at the bottom. No one knew for sure whether the Braves could keep up the pace, but they surely were the talk of the baseball world as May came to a close.

"Can this team win?" asked third sacker Terry Pendleton, anticipating the question that was on everyone's mind. "I certainly think it can compete. By July or August, we'll see how we're doing after we lose three in a row or go through a rough period. That's when you can tell if a team is ready."

There was little comparison between the 1990 Braves who'd finished last and this current version. At the end of May the staff ERA was still under 3.00. In 1990 it was 4.58, worst in the league. The ballclub also had the worst fielding average in '90, but the addition of Pendleton, Belliard and Bream to the infield had changed that as well.

The Braves had also gotten quite an infusion of speed. In 1990 they'd ranked last in stolen bases with 92. Now, led by Otis Nixon, they had already accumulated 45 and were keeping a pace that would come out to 228 steals for the season. More and more people were coming to regard them as contenders rather than pretenders.

Referring to the Braves' surprising start, veteran Cubs manager Don Zimmer said, "If you've got young guys and they start winning a few games, they get to feeling they can beat anybody."

But the overall feeling was that a number of things would have to go the Braves' way for them to win. The consensus was that the team would eventually have to find a reliable fifth starter, would need one of the relievers to emerge as the closer, would need the middle of the lineup to continue providing power and would need help from the other teams in the division. Both the Reds (the defending champs) and the Dodgers would have to regress somewhat and put together a less than super season. But in baseball, stranger things have happened. As General Manager John Schuerholz said, "I have this new, juiced-up feeling."

So did the rest of the Braves.

The Twins

The Twins had also made some surprise moves before their season began. They released second sacker Nelson Liriano and gave the job to a rookie named Chuck Knoblauch. Decisions like that can be risky if the rookie flops. The club was also worried about the hitting of Mike Pagliarulo, who had just a .163 average in 13 pre-season games. As insurance, they decided to keep young shortstop Scott Leius and give him some time at third.

"I don't mind going from the 'shortstop of the future' to the 'third baseman of the future,'" said Leius, "as long as the next move isn't 'bullpen catcher of the future.'"

One plus was the spring hitting of newly acquired Chili Davis. Davis had 6 homers and 17 RBI's in his first 63 spring at bats, giving the team a power-hitting designated hitter who could swing the bat from either side of the plate. They wouldn't have to platoon in that spot.

Overall, the Twins had made fewer changes than the Braves. Knoblauch was the new second sacker; Pagliarulo and Leius would platoon at third, while Davis moved in at designated hitter. On the mound, the two most important newcomers were Jack Morris and Steve Bedrosian. Young Scott Erickson had moved into the rotation, joining Morris, Allan Anderson, Tapani and young Mark Guthrie. David West went on the disabled list just before the season began.

The season didn't open on a high note for the Twins. The team played six games the first week and won just a pair. Two high spots were a seven-hit, nine-strikeout shutout by Tapani and a nice performance by Anderson, who allowed just a run in seven and a third innings of work. Erickson also pitched well, giving up just one run in seven innings of work. But he lost the game. Morris, however, found himself getting lit up twice, losing his first two starts and doing it to the tune of a 9.58 ERA. Southpaw Guthrie was really racked up in his first start. When he came out his ERA stood at 23.14. That's out of sight.

Morris, after pitching the opener, which he lost 7–2 to Dave Stewart and the defending champ A's, thought he was too psyched up.

"I didn't stay within myself," the veteran said. "There was some extra adrenaline. I don't think it was because I was pitching for a different team."

Morris's performance in his first two outings had to be of some immediate concern because of critics who said the 36-year-old was on the downside. If he failed to emerge as the leader of the staff, a guy everyone could depend on in the big games, the young pitchers would be more inclined to feel the bite of big-time pressure.

Of greater concern was the lack of hitting by both Dan Gladden and Shane Mack. Gladden was off to a 1-for-21 start in six games, while Mack was just 1-for-13. Hrbek was also struggling with 3-for-23, a .130 average. But the big guy still managed a team-leading 5 RBI's. On the plus side, rookie Knoblauch was hitting .400 on an 8-for-20 start and seemed to have taken the second base job by the horns. Puckett and Davis were also hitting. But overall it was still too early to make a real judgment about the improvement of the ballclub.

By the end of the next week, however, some believed that a judgment could be made. The Twins had plummeted into last place with a 2–9 start that might have spelled disaster. With a .210 team average, there just wasn't enough hitting. Morris lost his third straight game, both Scott Erickson and Allan Anderson were at 1–2, and the pitchers in general were feeling the pinch of no support. They were already thinking they had to throw a shutout to win.

"It's nothing to get concerned about yet," said pitching coach Dick Such. "But if it goes on for a while, it might be."

Fortunately, the slump went no further. The club won six of its next seven, with Morris taking two of the victories. Now the team had a .262 batting average, with several starters hitting very well, especially rookie Knoblauch and veterans Puckett, Brian Harper and Chili Davis. That took some of the pressure off those who were still trying to get untracked.

As usual, the Twins were playing their best ball at the Metrodome. They were 7–3 at home with a .330 batting average. On the road they were just 2–7 and hitting only .181 as a team. The club would have to win more on the road if it hoped to get back into contention.

During the next two weeks the Twins continued to play good baseball, inching above the .500 mark. When they upped their record to 16–15, it marked the first time the ballclub had gone over .500 since June 14, 1990. Whether or not they would be a contender still wasn't a certainty, but the Twins did not look like a last-place team in 1991.

The team had also discovered a hot pitcher. Right-hander Scott Erickson, who had pitched so well after being called up in June 1990, began showing everyone he was for real. Erickson, who had left the University of Arizona less than two years earlier, had jumped from Double A ball in Orlando right to the Twins and promptly posted the lowest ERA (2.87) for a Minnesota rookie since Doug Corbett back in 1980.

At 6'4", 225 pounds, Erickson was a menacing figure on the mound. He was an intense competitor who glared at hitters, then threw a moving fastball and nasty slider. He had lost two early-season games when the Twins failed to score a run for him. Otherwise, he was simply overpowering. When he threw eight scoreless innings in a victory over the Red Sox on May 7, he had pitched 30 straight scoreless frames to tie a club record set by Frank Viola.

Next, the big righty worked seven more scoreless innings in a defeat of the Tigers to run his record to 5–2 and lower his ERA to a microscopic 1.45. Veteran catcher Junior Ortiz called Erickson "the hardest pitcher I've ever caught because his ball moves so much."

Kirby Puckett called the 23-year-old pitcher "Superman" because he resembled actor Christopher Reeve, who played the Man of Steel in the movies. But the way Erickson had been pitching, "Superman" could have been a nickname earned for his mound exploits.

At the end of the sixth week, the Twins were in sixth place, still struggling to stay above .500 at 19–18. But their place in the standings was deceiving. For openers, six of the seven teams in the A.L. West were playing above .500. In addition, only a game and a half separated the Rangers, Angels, White Sox and Twins. And

Minnesota trailed division-leading Oakland by just three and a half games. So as May wound down, the Twins were still jockeying for position in a very competitive and balanced division. Most observers, however, still believed the defending champion A's would eventually break away from the pack.

And the Twins still had questions, most of them concerning the pitching staff. Erickson was now 6–2 with a 1.44 ERA. He was close to perfect and thus far perhaps the best pitcher in the American League. Aguilera was also looking sharp as a closer. He already had seven saves and a 1.62 ERA. The veteran Bedrosian had a pair of saves, a 2–1 record and a 2.82 ERA. But after that, there were problems.

Tapani had fallen to 2–3 and his ERA had risen to 3.00. Lefty Mark Guthrie had a 3–2 record but a fat 5.01 ERA. And the two veterans, Morris and Anderson, had both been inconsistent. Morris still didn't look like the veteran stopper the club had hoped he'd be. He was 3–5 with a 5.34 ERA. Worse yet, when he returned to Tiger Stadium to pitch against his old club, he was completely ineffective. Detroit scored seven first-inning runs off the veteran, as he was touched for a three-run homer by Cecil Fielder and a grand slam by rookie Milt Cuyler.

Anderson was 1–3 with a 4.80 ERA. He had performed like Dr. Jekyll and Mr. Hyde. In four

The Heroes of
"The Worst to First Season of the
Atlanta Braves and Minnesota Twins"

Jeff Treadway, the Braves' second baseman and chief
pinch hitter, hit .320 during the regular season.

Kent Hrbek, launching one of his twenty homers hit during the season, was the finest fielding first baseman in the game.

Chuck Knoblauch is considered the 1991 Rookie of the Year, pictured here slapping a single in the Pennant Drive.

Rick Aguilera was obtained two years ago from the New York Mets in the Viola trade, and helped the Twins to the top with forty-two saves during the season and two in the Series.

Hitting a dramatic home run in the sixth game of the Series in the 11th inning, Kirby Puckett is truly the heart and soul of the Twins.

Chili Davis, like his name, was hot through the entire year, leading the Twins in home runs (29) and RBIs (93), with two round-trippers in the Fall Classic.

Greg Gagne is the glue for the Twins' infield. He only made nine errors in the entire season, and had a perfect Series in the field.

Kevin Tapani, part of the infamous Viola trade, was a 16-game-winning righthander, and shone in the League Championship Series with Toronto.

Dan Gladden gladdened Twins' Fans' hearts all season, igniting the Twins' offense.

The Twins' Shane "Mack the Knife" Mack had a
career year in 1991. Here he is attempting to steal
second base.

One of the true characters and dominant pitchers
to emerge recently, Scott Erikson has a consistent
92mph fastball.

21-year-old southpaw, Steve Avery, showed his mettle by winning 18 games during the regular season. He was the dominant factor against the Pirates in the League Championship.

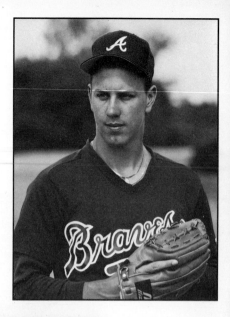

Greg Olson, Braves catcher, was the spark-plug for the team in the League Championship and the Series.

Sid Bream split time at first base during the season, hitting against his old teammates during the League championship series.

Ron Gant, the Atlanta Braves' "30/30" Man, looking to steal again.

20-game winning southpaw for the Braves, Tom Glavine.

David Justice, despite missing six weeks during the season, displays "the sweetest swing in baseball".

1991 Hitting Champ and MVP Candidate, Terry
Pendleton, hit a career-high twenty-two home runs.

The only non-Yankee to ever hit three homers in three consecutive games of the World Series, Lonnie Smith has also been in five World Series in ten years.

John Smoltz, the majors' hottest pitcher after the All-Star Break, went 12 and 12 in the second half of the season.

From WORST to FIRST Record
ATLANTA BRAVES

YEAR	WINS	LOSS	PCT.
1990	65	97	.401
1991	94	68	.580

From WORST to FIRST Record
MINNESOTA TWINS

YEAR	WINS	LOSS	PCT.
1990	74	88	.457
1991	95	67	.586

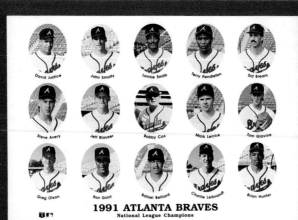

David Justice · John Smoltz · Lonnie Smith · Terry Pendleton · Sid Bream

Steve Avery · Jeff Blauser · Bobby Cox · Mark Lemke · Tom Glavine

Greg Olson · Ron Gant · Rafael Belliard · Charlie Leibrandt · Brian Hunter

1991 ATLANTA BRAVES
National League Champions

Kirby Puckett · Jack Morris · Chili Davis · Shane Mack · Chuck Knoblauch

Scott Erickson · Greg Gagne · Tom Kelly · Kent Hrbek · Mike Pagliarulo

Randy Bush · Kevin Tapani · Rick Aguilera · Dan Gladden · Brian Harper

1991 MINNESOTA TWINS
World Champions

good starts he was 1–0 with a 1.53 ERA. But in four bad starts, his numbers read 0–3 and 10.91 ERA. Would the real Allan Anderson please stand up? Even Manager Kelly wasn't sure about the two veteran hurlers.

"When you're driving to the ballpark, you like to have a feeling you're going to win," Kelly said. "With Andy and Jack, we don't know what to expect."

The hitting was more promising. Catcher Harper had been on a tear and had his average up to .372. Rookie outfielder Pedro Munoz, who was hitting .408 at Portland in the Pacific Coast League, had been called up and hit .333 in his first 24 at bats. Rookie Knoblauch continued to excel and was at .313, while Puckett checked in at .310. Shortstop Gagne was overachieving at .308, while designated hitter Davis was hitting .293 with a team-leading 8 homers and 23 RBI's. Hrbek, Gladden, Mack and young Leius were all struggling, but the team batting average of .274 was good.

Very few people were calling the Twins contenders as yet. The main reason was the overwhelming respect everyone still had for the A's, who were trying for a fourth consecutive division title. But the Twins had already shown they were once again a team to be reckoned with, a team with plenty of firepower and, in the early going, a young superpitcher.

Chapter Six

On to the All-Star Break

The month and a half leading up to the All-Star break is an important time for teams to establish themselves, to set the tone for what will follow in the second half of the season. Sure, plenty of teams have made stretch runs, coming from nowhere after the break. But most clubs like to maneuver themselves into a position from which they can make a move.

With teams like the Braves and Twins, the period before the All-Star break was even more important. Both clubs were trying to establish themselves as contenders, shed the loser's image from the year before, and at the same time find the right chemistry between the older players and the newcomers. The feeling was the same with both teams. If they could hang tough to that midseason point, at least they would have a chance.

The Braves

The Braves were hanging tough. At the beginning of June a combination of youngsters and older pros were giving the team a good deal of its lift and keeping it on the topside of the .500 mark. In fact, just as the Twins had Scott Erickson, the Braves also had a pitcher who was performing as well as anyone in the league.

Lefty Tom Glavine had won five straight and was 7–2 on the year with a 2.13 ERA. He was getting 5–2 support from the 21-year-old Avery, who seemed a much more mature pitcher than the nervous kid who had gone 3–11 just a year earlier. The one sore spot was Smoltz, still struggling at 1–6. This was a guy with a super arm who had produced two winning seasons with bad teams. Now, with a much improved ballclub behind him, he was looking awful.

Young David Justice continued to tattoo National League pitching. He was hitting over .300 and his 32 RBI's were third best in the league. Pendleton was hitting .343, Treadway .341, the surprising Nixon .333 with 16 steals. Bream was up to .265, but also had 5 homers and 24 ribbies.

And while Gant continued to struggle with an average below .200, he still had a team-leading 6 home runs.

There was one personnel move of note at the beginning of June. Because of Otis Nixon's fine play, Deion Sanders was optioned to Richmond of the International League. Shortly afterward, the team also brought up a young first baseman named Brian Hunter to give Bream an occasional day off.

During the next two weeks, more and more people began thinking that these Braves were for real. Glavine continued to pitch outstanding baseball, running his record up to 10–2. "Look in his eyes and you can see the confidence," said his catcher, Greg Olson. Justice continued his hot hitting with an average of .333 whenever runners were in scoring position. Jeff Blauser, given a chance to see some action, went 9 for 13 with 3 homers and 12 RBI's. That's the mark of a good team: players coming through whenever they have the opportunity.

Through June 9, the Braves were 29–23, six games over .500 and in second place, just a game and a half behind front-running Los Angeles. Though the team's pace would slow over the following weeks, there always seemed to be someone on the Braves coming up with a great individual performance.

For instance, pitcher Avery not only whipped

the Mets, 6–1, with a complete game performance, but he also got four hits during the course of the game. "Every time I got a hit, I was surprised," he said afterward. "I know I'm not going to go out and make a living hitting."

Then in a game at Montreal, Otis Nixon set a National League record by stealing six bases. "He really put on a clinic out there," said the Expos' Marquis Grissom, himself a top base thief.

Next it was rookie Brian Hunter's turn. Since coming up from Richmond and playing as a fill-in for Bream, Hunter had 11 RBI's on his first 11 hits. Four of them were home runs.

There was also evidence that the team was coming together in other ways. In a game with the Phillies, Roger McDowell plunked Nixon with a pitch. When Glavine returned to the mound he found himself facing former teammate Dale Murphy. Glavine promptly threw four straight pitches way inside to Murphy. The result was that both Glavine and McDowell were ejected from the game.

"The bottom line is you've got to try to protect your players," Glavine said. "If it was a different hitter up there, something different might have happened."

On the downside, John Smoltz continued to struggle, prompting Manager Cox to consider a move to the bullpen. "We've always thought he'd make a good closer," Cox said. The closer was an element the team lacked.

There were also the first signs of injury, something every good team must face. The third week in June, a sore back made Justice miss four games, and Bream had to sit out six with an old problem, an injured knee. That was part of the reason the team fell back at the end of June. The Braves were now in third place with a 37–36 record, seven and a half games behind front-running Los Angeles and three and a half behind second-place Cincinnati.

It was also announced that Glavine had been fined $200 for his brushback pitches to Murphy. But the real bad news was that both Justice and Bream had been placed on the 15-day disabled list. With the team slumping, those injuries couldn't have come at a worse time. Add to that slumps by Ron Gant (1-for-20), Tommy Gregg (1-for-23) and Greg Olson (1-for-20) and it was no surprise that the club was almost back at .500.

Steve Avery, for one, believed the pitchers would have to pick up some of the slack while the offense suffered. "I know we're going to have to perk us up while David [Justice] and Sid [Bream] are out," he said. "Our whole staff is trying to pick it up a notch."

The first week in July the ballclub fell below .500 at 39–40 and was nine and a half games off the pace. It was All-Star break time, the season roughly half over. There was little doubt that the resumption of play would be a crucial time for the Braves. A poor start after the break and they were in trouble. Everyone knew it.

A look at the midseason stats didn't profile a losing team. The Braves were second in hitting, one point behind the Cards at .263. They had also scored the most runs in the league. The pitching wasn't too far behind, the staff ERA of 3.62 fourth best in the league.

Pendleton was tied for second in the batting race at .324. The free-agent pickup was having a great year after his dismal 1990 season with the Cards. Gant was among the league leaders in home runs with 15, while Nixon led in stolen bases with 42.

Treadway was hitting .333 in a part-time role, while Nixon was having a career year, batting .314 to go with all the steals. He had become the perfect lead-off man. Young Brian Hunter had filled in for the injured Bream to the tune of a .314 average. Blauser was hitting a solid .280 with 7 homers and 36 ribbies, also in a part-time role. Gant was up to .239 and 44 homers to go with his 15 homers. Justice had 11 homers and a team-leading 51 RBI's before going down with back problems.

On the mound the big news continued to be Tom Glavine. At the All-Star break the left-hander had a 12–4 mark and a 1.98 ERA and was considered the best pitcher in the league. He was also second to David Cone of the Mets in strikeouts with 108. It was a dream season for him. But if it was a dream season for Glavine, it was a nightmare for John Smoltz.

The right-hander with as much "stuff" as any pitcher in the league was mired at 2–11 with a 5.16 ERA. No matter what he tried, he couldn't seem to turn things around.

"I definitely feel I let the team down, myself and a lot of people as well," a disconsolate Smoltz said. "I've got to prove to everybody that I can be the dominating pitcher everybody wants me to be—and says I can be because of the stuff I have."

In between Glavine and Smoltz there was Avery. The kid with the 90-plus-mph fastball was rapidly learning his craft and had an 8–5 record during the first half of the season. His ERA of 3.96 was high, but he seemed to be getting better. Leibrandt was holding his own at 7–7. Berenguer with 12 saves; Mercker with a 4–3 record, a 1.78 ERA and 4 saves; and Mike Stanton with a 3–1 mark were doing the job out of the pen. Berenguer wasn't a classic closer, but was the best the team had.

Glavine started the All-Star Game for the National League and pitched two scoreless innings. He was the Braves' only representative. The American League won it, 4–2, and all the players returned to their teams for the second half of the season. If the Braves were going to make a move, it would have to be soon.

The Twins

Things were not looking very good for the Minnesota Twins. On May 19, the club had moved within three games of first place, but then promptly lost six of seven games. By May 26, the team was back in sixth place with a 20–23 mark, six and a half games behind first-place Texas. All seven teams in the division were within seven and a half games of each other, but the Twins seemed to be headed downward.

Too many players were either slumping or just not producing. Kent Hrbek, for instance, was hitting just .223 with five extra base hits. The 250-pound first sacker had a slugging percentage of just .298.

"I have to just keep working, plugging, churning," Hrbek said. "It's my turn to start doing something. There have been so many times when runners were on base and one hit would have made the difference. I just haven't been able to get that hit."

FROM WORST TO FIRST!

Rookie Knoblauch was in a 7-for-40 skid that dropped his average from .336 to .294. Right-hander Tapani hadn't won a game since April 27. Some of the players from the year before remembered that 7–21 skid in June that all but finished their season.

"I don't think the same thing is going to happen," said Brian Harper. "We know we're too good for that to happen again."

Among the pitchers, only Erickson and Aguilera were consistent and effective. Morris, however, was showing signs of life at 4–5, and the team still hoped he would emerge as the staff leader. Harper, Puckett, Davis, rookie Munoz and Gagne were all over the .300 mark. The Twins were still second in hitting with a .273 average, but they weren't hitting in the clutch and weren't scoring enough runs.

On the morning of June 1, the Twins were 23–25. That night they whipped Kansas City, 8–4, behind Allan Anderson's second win. The next day Erickson pitched the club to a 4–1 victory over Kansas City once more. It was the youngster's eighth victory of the year and evened the club's record at 25–25 once more. And while the Twins were only at .500, they were just four and a half games out of first and sitting in fifth place.

The following week the Twins played six games. The log read like this: A 3–2 victory over

From Worst to First!

Baltimore as Morris finally got above .500 at
6–5. In 10 innings, the Twins whipped the Orioles again, 4–3, as the club banged out 13 hits.
A second straight win, 4–3, over the O's as Tapani raised his record to 3–6 and Aguilera saved
his 13th. A 2–0 shutout of Cleveland as Anderson and Aguilera combined for the whitewash.
A second straight win over the Indians, this time
by a 2–1 count as Erickson raised his record to
9–2 and Aggie saved his 15th. Then Cleveland
fell again, 9–2, as Morris went eight innings in
raising his record to 7–5.

Suddenly the Twins had an eight-game win
streak, their longest since 1985 when they won
10 straight. They were 31–25, in third place, and
just three and a half behind Oakland. But they
didn't stop there. The next week they won all
seven games they played, beginning with another victory over Cleveland. Next they
whipped the Yanks three straight behind Tapani, Anderson and Erickson, who won his
10th. From there it was on to Cleveland for three
more wins. Morris threw a shutout to raise his
record to 8–5. The next was an 11–7 barnburner
as the club pounded out 15 hits and Scott Leius
drove home four runs. And finally they took a
4–2, 10-inning victory over the Tribe as Aguilera
won it in relief of Tapani.

From out of nowhere, the Twins had won 15
straight games, the longest streak in the majors

71

since the Royals had won 16 straight back in 1977. They were the hottest team in baseball. On June 16, the ballclub had run its record to 38–25. But that wasn't the big news. The big news was that the Minnesota Twins had taken over first place in the American League West, jumping over the Oakland A's and leading the pack by half a game. The players and Manager Kelly were ecstatic.

Though everyone had contributed to the streak, one of the biggest turnarounds was the pitching of Morris. He had won six of his last seven starts, all to the tune of a 1.86 ERA.

"I'm rejuvenated," he said. "Without sounding like Mr. Negative, I don't think they ever knew me in Detroit, or recognized what I accomplished."

In other words, he was happy to be in Minnesota. His manager was also happy he was there.

"We needed a guy like Jack," said Tom Kelly. "The last couple of years here, one pitcher would look at another and say, 'How about you taking care of it today?' The other guy would say, 'How about you taking care of it?' Jack takes care of it. He takes the pressure off Erickson, Tapani and the other young guys."

Despite their sudden ascendance to the top of the division, the Twins were careful not to get overexcited. As Kirby Puckett said, "Most teams would be jumping up and down. Not us. We know this game can humble you."

Everyone seemed to contribute to the streak. The ballclub was now leading the American League in hitting with a .278 average. In fact, it was leading the majors. That wasn't all. The Twins' pitchers now had a league-low 3.47 ERA. So they also had the top pitching staff. How could they not be taken seriously now?

"The Twins are good," said Blue Jays scout Gordon Lakey. "They'll be a factor all year."

Indians pitching coach Mark Willey noted that besides being at the top in hitting and pitching, the team excelled in yet another area. "Their defense is so underrated," said Willey. "If they stay healthy, they're in good shape."

And infielder Al Newman, who'd been part of the world champion Twins of four years earlier, said bluntly, "I think this team is, overall, much better than the eighty-seven team."

Of course, nothing lasts forever. The streak ended when the Orioles whipped the Twins, 6–5, getting three runs in the ninth off Aguilera. Only the ballclub quickly showed it wasn't about to fade. The team quickly bounced back to win four of the next five, and going into the final week of June had moved out to a three-game lead over Oakland. Things were looking even better.

The following week Morris won his eighth

straight game to run his record to 11–5. Erickson, however, finally lost after 12 straight victories. He also reported some soreness in his right elbow. The team said he might miss a start and could even be held out of the All-Star Game. Whenever a young pitcher reports soreness in his elbow or shoulder, people get nervous. Erickson was such a valuable commodity that no one wanted to take a chance.

Before the break the team suffered a small letdown, losing five of seven. That dropped it back into a virtual tie with Texas, though the Rangers were percentage points ahead. The Twins were at 47–36, their first-half performance surprising everyone. Even Manager Kelly was optimistic.

"We have a chance to win this thing if we stay healthy and do things fundamentally right," he said.

But Kelly was not without worries as the team prepared for the All-Star hiatus. The Twins had been virtually injury-free during the first half of the season. Now some problems were developing. On the disabled list were both Gene Larkin (with a pulled groin) and Dan Gladden (with strained abdominal muscles). They were quickly followed by a third, and this one had everyone worried.

Not wanting to take a chance on such a valuable commodity, the Twins also placed Scott

Erickson on the DL. They didn't want the young-ster to rush back from his sore elbow. Erickson, however, believed the problem was already be-hind him. He said he had received a call from his former coach at the University of Arizona, Jim Wing. Wing said he spotted a flaw in the pitcher's delivery that might be causing his el-bow problems.

"It had to do with the angle of my arm when I pull it out of the glove," explained Erickson. "I feel real good about things now."

At the All-Star break, Harper and Puckett con-tinued to hit over .300. Davis led the team with 19 homers and 52 RBI's. Hrbek was up to .281 with 42 ribbies, and rookie Knoblauch contin-ued to play well. Erickson was 12–3 with a 1.83 ERA, while Morris had rebounded to 11–6. Aguilera had 22 saves. The secondary starters were still struggling, but things seemed in place for a good second half.

Morris was the starting pitcher in the All-Star Game, throwing two innings in the American League's victory. Aguilera pitched one and two-thirds innings of relief, while Puckett saw action behind Ken Griffey, Jr., in center. Then it was back to business. The dog days of August lay ahead, and the Twins were trying to win a di-visional title. Come to think of it, someone remarked, if they did win they would become the first team ever to go from last one year to first the next.

That gave the ballclub yet another goal.

Chapter Seven

Through the Dog Days

For centuries, the month of August has been known as the dog days, and is usually the hottest month in most major-league cities. Back when there were all-day games, in the days before air-conditioned, domed stadiums, the August heat could be brutal, often wearing down players and teams.

August is also a dead spot in the baseball season. It isn't quite time for a stretch drive, the excitement of the All-Star Game has passed, and for teams out of the race, getting motivated can be a problem. It wasn't that way for the Braves and the Twins in 1991. Both teams were in the thick of a divisional race. To stay there, they would have to remain healthy and keep playing well throughout late July and into the dog days.

The Braves

The Braves started the second half of the season with mixed signals. There was no doubt that they were in the race, and they hoped they were in to stay. They continued to hang tough even without David Justice and Sid Bream. The two were still disabled. Bream was recovering from arthroscopic knee surgery and Justice's back continued to puzzle everyone.

"It's not playable," Justice said of his back. "If I try to play I know I'll be back to square one. It's frustrating."

Now there were more injury woes. Catcher Mike Heath, one of the team's free-agent signees, underwent surgery to remove bone chips from his right elbow and would probably be lost for the season. That left Greg Olson the only experienced catcher on the roster. Catcher/first baseman Francisco Cabrera was brought up, but he only had four games of big-league catching experience.

The ballclub was hoping another problem might be on the way to being solved. Pitcher John Smoltz, who had suffered through that humiliating 2–11 first half, was taking an unusual approach to his dilemma. He began meeting with a sports psychologist and promptly pitched the team to a 6–2 win over St. Louis. It was his first victory since May 30.

Smoltz said he spoke with the psychologist the day before he pitched, then again a few hours before the start. "He worked with me on my mental approach and it helped," Smoltz explained. "He gave me positive reinforcement and some little drills you can work within yourself."

The Braves were hoping it would keep working. If Smoltz could regain his form of the past two years, his efforts combined with Glavine's and Avery's could help pitch the team to a title. The other two youngsters continued to win. Glavine took his 13th; then Avery went out and whipped the Cards, 4–1, in a performance that saw him retire the first 18 St. Louis hitters. For a 21-year-old, the hard-throwing southpaw was impressing a lot of people.

"That could be the best performance I've caught by anybody this year," said Avery's catcher, Greg Olson.

Otis Nixon also broke the club record for steals when he swiped his 43rd base, and Manager Cox was given a two-year contract extension for the job he had done behind the bench. In addition, the team went over the million mark in attendance, the earliest date on which it had passed that milestone since 1983.

It didn't hurt that the team was still winning. The first week after the All-Star break the club won six of seven games and chopped six full games off the slumping Dodgers' lead. Now the Braves trailed by just three. Third baseman Pendleton continued on fire. His average was up to .338 and he already had 10 homers and 42 RBI's. A free agent coming off his worse season, Pendleton was suddenly putting together a career year.

Perhaps the most frustrated Brave was David Justice. His bad back still wasn't coming around. "I was such a big part of the team the first half that I feel bad I can't help us now," he said. "I was relied on to produce. The pain isn't like it was. At least I can walk better now. Before I couldn't even walk that well."

The Braves took the chase into August. On July 28, they had fallen to six behind L.A. The Braves were 49–46, in second place. The defending champion Reds were third at 47–49, but they somehow didn't appear to be a team that could repeat. The Padres and Giants were both streaky, while the Astros were out of it. Most experts favored the Dodgers. Some still weren't taking the Braves seriously.

The best news was probably the transformation of Smoltz. He won his third straight game

of the second half, his third game since beginning to see the psychologist. No one was complaining about his methods now. Avery was also
getting better, running his record to 11–5 and
drawing more praise from catcher Olson.

"At this point last year he was a stubborn,
hard-headed kid," said Olson. "He just wanted
to do the things that got him to the major leagues,
rather than improve on the stuff he already had.
He's no longer just a hard thrower. He's becoming a pitcher."

Avery was now just two wins behind Glavine
and joked about it. "Tom is keeping me in the
background so I can sneak up on people," he
said.

As the dog days began, every week seemed a
new adventure for almost every team in the division. The Braves had gone from three games
back to six. The next week they came back to
three and a half. They weren't letting the Dodgers get away. They also picked up veteran right-
hander Jim Clancy to bolster the pitching staff
and activated Sid Bream to replace Deion Sanders, who had been recalled after the All-Star
break but was now leaving to join the football
Falcons.

By August 11, things were getting interesting.
The Braves had pulled to within one and a half
games of L.A. The Dodgers were at 61–49, the
Braves 59–50. A sweep of the Astros brought the

Braves nine games over .500, the first time they had been that far on the plus side since June 21, 1984.

In a reversal of roles, Glavine had gone into a small slump, losing three of four games to drop to 14–7—but Smoltz was 6–1 since the break and now 8–12 for the year. He was looking as strong as any pitcher in the league. The turnaround couldn't have come at a better time.

"I was tired of being the first one dressed and ready to leave when I pitched," Smoltz said. "I know how good I can be. It was frustrating early in the season, but it sure is rewarding now."

Justice also believed he was almost ready to return. "I expect to be rusty," he said. "But I'll tell you something: I'm going to be aggressive when I get in there."

But Justice still wasn't ready the next week. Though the Braves stayed within one and a half, they suddenly lost Juan Berenguer to an arm injury. With their top closer on the disabled list, the club recalled right-hander Mark Wohlers, a big fastballer, from Richmond. But now the team might have to look for a stopper.

It seemed, however, that no matter what happened the Braves hung in there. By August 25, the team was within a game of the Dodgers. The Reds, Giants and Padres appeared to be out of it. The race had come down to just two teams, one of which had been a distant last the year before. As was happening in Minnesota, fans soon became aware that no team had ever jumped from last to first. That was added incentive for the Braves and their increasingly exuberant fans.

In the thick of the pennant race, Atlanta continued to make personnel changes. Justice finally came off the DL and had seven hits including a homer and four RBI's his first week back. As he said, he had come back ripping and slashing. Berenguer received a cortisone shot in the hope that he could come off the DL. Reliever Kent Mercker was also reactivated after sitting out with a pulled muscle in his side. Glavine sprained an ankle sliding, but was expected to pitch with a brace on the ankle. Smoltz had to leave a game with a cramp in his right leg, but he was now 9–13.

Rookie Brian Mitchell, up from the minors, was hitting .373 in his first 51 at bats. Rookie Brian Hunter had 10 homers and 40 RBI's, while Gant was up over .250 with 27 homers and 78 ribbies, as well as 25 steals. He was putting together another fine year. Nixon was up to 67 steals, leading the majors by far. Even the veteran Leibrandt had won three straight starts to bring his record to 12–11. The Braves were exhibiting a characteristic of all great teams: whenever somebody faltered, there was somebody else to pick up the slack.

FROM WORST TO FIRST!

The dog days of August were finally over. After the games of September 1, the Braves and the Dodgers were tied. They had identical records, 72–58. It really looked as if the two teams were going to battle down to the wire. Glavine won his 17th game to make him the top winner in the majors. But he had help. Avery was 14–8, Leibrandt 13–11 and Smoltz 10–13, 8–2 since the All-Star break.

In addition, the Braves made a trade that was considered a minor one at first. They sent relief pitcher Tony Castillo and a minor-leaguer to the New York Mets in return for veteran right-hander Alejandro Pena. Pena was acquired as a fifth starter, but the club would soon find a new, important role for the fastballing vet.

With the dog days over, it was almost crunch time. September 1 was the first day of the stretch run. It would be the Braves and Dodgers battling for the title—and also to see if Atlanta could become the first team to go from worst to first.

The Twins

Minnesota wasted no time taking charge after the All-Star break. The Twins promptly won three straight from Boston and by week's end were back in first, two games in front of Texas. The Twins' hitting was now pretty much a constant, but the pitching still posed some questions.

Jack Morris had rebounded from his poor start and was now a 12–6 pitcher, once again up among the mound elite in the league. Erickson, however, was still on the disabled list, though he said his elbow was coming around. Allan Anderson, inconsistent all year at 4–7, was bumped from the rotation and was being evaluated. And Kevin Tapani, a disappointment at 5–7, was complaining that he had hurt his arm by sleeping in the wrong position.

The major worry, of course, was Erickson. The big right-hander had made a tremendous impression on the entire league during the first half of the season. For a pitcher with just a few months of big-league experience, he had come on like a house afire, a combination of confidence and intensity.

Said the veteran Morris, "I've seen a lot of talented players who don't do anything in baseball because they don't have heart. Scott has heart. You can teach fundamentals and you can teach mechanics, but you can't teach heart. He's intense."

Erickson liked to dress all in black on days he pitched. Even his glove and shoes were black.

During a game he was pitching he just sat alone at the end of the bench between innings, deep in concentration. Even the veteran Kirby Puckett marveled at the youngster's concentration. "On days he pitches, no one goes near the guy," said Puckett.

Teammate Kevin Tapani referred to Erickson's turn in the rotation as "the Day of Death." No wonder the team was concerned about his tender elbow.

Erickson returned the next week and in his first start was given an 8–1 lead but couldn't last long enough to hold it. He won his second start to run his record to 13–3, throwing seven scoreless innings. Manager Kelly, however, wasn't sure the youngster was all the way back.

"We have all seen Scott pitch better, but he's coming along," Kelly said. "Maybe a couple more starts and he'll be back to his old self."

The good news was that by July 21, the Twins had increased their lead to five and a half games over both Texas and Chicago. Their record was 55–38 and getting better. Third sacker Mike Pagliarulo, a guy many people had thought was finished, had been on a tear and had his average up to .291. Shane Mack was also starting to hit and Chili Davis had 20 homers and 61 RBI's. Someone kept picking up the slack.

By the first week in August the Twins were 20 games over .500 at 63–43. They now had the best winning percentage in the entire major leagues, but led the White Sox by only three games. Kevin Tapani had become a hot pitcher, raising his record to 8–7 with a 2.97 ERA. And Shane Mack continued on a hitting tear, having raised his average from .242 to .300 in the course of a month. But while Erickson was 15–3, his ERA was going up and the Twins' management thought he was still babying the elbow, even though the doctors had pronounced it healthy.

"He has been letting his mind wander and that's not like him," said pitching coach Dick Such. "There are only two ways he can go now. Either he decides to go on the DL again and rest the elbow for the rest of the year, or he goes out and throws the baseball."

Despite worrying about Erickson, the team was enjoying the fact that the rest of the division was chasing it. Confidence was growing. As reliever Rick Aguilera said, "I think we've proven now that we're for real, that this isn't some fluke team in first place."

On August 11, the race had tightened. The Twins had a 67–45 record, but the White Sox were red hot and within a game of the top. Oakland was also showing signs of life, trailing by just three. There were still many who figured the A's were the team that would ultimately get hot and take over the top spot. Tapani was at 10–7, but Morris had lost three of four to go

13–9. Erickson had his worst inning as a pro in an 8–0 loss to Seattle. The right-hander gave up five runs on five hits and two walks. Just four batters into the game the bullpen was at work. Whether the Twins could win without an effective Erickson was still a matter of conjecture.

By August 18, however, the lead was back to three and a half over the White Sox and a surprising seven over the fading A's. A week later it began to look as if the Twins were not only weathering the dog days, but were actually flourishing. Now the White Sox were fading, and on the 25th the Twins had a seven-game lead over both the Pale Hose and the A's. At 75–51, they continued to play the best ball in the big leagues.

Though Erickson's record was still an impressive 16–6, the numbers clearly indicated he was not the same pitcher now that he'd been in the first half of the season. The young right-hander had peaked on June 29, his record at 12–2 with a 1.39 ERA. It was pointed up that since then he was 4–4 with a 7.83 ERA. Something still seemed wrong, though the club insisted it wasn't his elbow. No one seemed to have an answer.

On September 1, the Twins appeared to be firmly in control of the division. They continued to show the best record in baseball and now had an eight-game lead over Oakland. The A's, the

From Worst to First!

White Sox, Texas, Kansas City, Seattle—all within three and a half games of each other, none seemed to have enough firepower to mount a serious September charge. Barring a complete collapse, the Twins seemed almost certain to complete their worst-to-first odyssey.

With a month to go, the Twins led the majors in hitting with an impressive .284 team average. They were still third in pitching and looking good. Erickson was held out of the rotation for a week and still at 16–6. But a hot Tapani was up to 13–7 and Morris had climbed to 16–10. And just about everyone was hitting. With the stretch run about to begin, utility infielder Al Newman perhaps put it best.

"We kind of have some leeway now," he said. "We're fortunate enough to be in a position where we can have a bad streak and still survive it."

Chapter Eight

The Stretch Run

This is the time that separates the men from the boys. More than once, teams that have seemed to have a lock on a title have wilted in the final weeks to finish also-rans. And teams that are battling for the brass ring often have to sustain the momentum right up to the final weekend of the year.

For the Braves and Twins the stretch run had different significance. Atlanta was still in a dogfight with the Dodgers. Either team could win it and neither could afford a letdown. It was the kind of race that often goes down to the final games. Minnesota, on the other hand, had a substantial lead and only had to sustain a good level of play to win. Their job was to do that while keeping everyone healthy and ready for the playoffs. Of course, they couldn't afford to look too far ahead. That can backfire also.

The Braves

The Braves and Dodgers stayed neck and neck through the first week of September. Injuries seemed to be the Braves' biggest worry. Utility man Jeff Blauser was the latest casualty, breaking a toe while completing a double play against the Expos. The team was still without Juan Berenguer, slow to recover from the injury to his forearm. Manager Cox continued to juggle his bullpen, still searching for the right guy for the right role.

If the Braves had any advantage at all, it was in the starting rotation. Both Leibrandt and Smoltz were hot; Glavine seemed to straighten himself out, and Avery had been consistent all year. The team was confident and playing without fear.

By mid-September, Atlanta had opened up a one-and-a-half-game lead. Any feeling that the young Braves might fold under the pressure was gone. This team was playing good baseball—period. The team proved it by taking the Dodgers two out of three. And that was after losing the first game.

Mike Morgan bested Glavine in the opener at Atlanta, 5–2. Once again the league's best pitcher in the first half of the season didn't look very sharp, giving up five runs in seven and a third innings of work. And the Braves got just five hits. So when Smoltz took the mound against Tim Belcher in the second game, it looked big. That one went 11 innings before the Braves won it, 3–2, the veteran Jim Clancy getting the win and Ron Gant the game-winning hit.

Then in the Sunday finale, young Steve Avery tossed a four-hitter and Sid Bream hit a first-inning grand slam off Ramon Martinez to key a 9–1 rout.

"A lot of people thought we would fold because we have a young team," Ron Gant said. "But I think we proved to everyone, including the Dodgers, that we can play well under pressure."

One pleasant surprise for the Braves had been the work of newcomer Alejandro Pena. Cox had begun using the hard-throwing right-hander as his closer and the veteran had responded, saving two games during the week and four since coming over from the Mets.

But nothing was settled yet. The Braves would have to endure yet another crisis, one that would once more test their mettle as a team. On September 16, a terse announcement came out of

Baseball Commissioner Fay Vincent's office. It said, in effect, that Braves outfielder Otis Nixon was being suspended for 60 days without pay for violating baseball's drug policy and his own aftercare program.

Nixon's original drug problem had begun before he came to the Braves. As was the league policy, he was tested periodically and when he failed a test, he was out. At this point, 60 days meant the rest of the season as well as any post-season play. At the time of his suspension, Nixon was in the midst of a career year, hitting .297 with a league-best 72 steals. His loss would be tough to take.

Shortly after his suspension, Nixon issued this statement: "I want to apologize to my teammates, the fans and the kids for letting them down at this time," it said. "It is tough for me right now, but I have made the right decisions and the problem and situations at hand are being dealt with."

Veteran Lonnie Smith was the man tapped to replace Nixon in left and in the lead-off spot. Smith had had his own battle with a drug problem years earlier and knew what his teammate was going through. He took exception to some of the wholesale criticism of Nixon.

"I know what it feels like," Smith said. "It's suffering; it's pain. People come up and say, 'Yeah, Lonnie, you were an addict, but you beat it. You beat cocaine. You're cured.' Let me tell you, the day I'm cured is the day I go to my grave. Every day is a battle."

Unfortunately, the baseball season can't stop for personal problems. The Braves had to go on, had to keep fighting for that divisional title. The players all knew it. David Justice said what many of the others were thinking.

"I'd be stupid to say we won't miss Otis," Justice said. "But when key guys have gone out, we've risen to the occasion. We can overcome it. We've been doing it all year."

That part was true. The Braves had survived the horrible first half by Smoltz. They had survived the loss of Justice and Bream, and the loss of Berenguer. No matter what, they had hung tough. Now, with the days dwindling down, they would have to absorb the loss of their offensive igniter, Otis Nixon.

The first two games after the suspension the club lost to San Francisco, 8–5 and 3–2. But it bounced back to whip the Padres twice, then headed into Los Angeles for a three-game showdown with the Dodgers. In the first one, Steve Avery went out and just blitzed through the Dodger lineup. He scattered six hits as the Braves won it, 3–0. In that one, Ron Gant belted his 30th home run, making him just the third player in baseball history to record back-to-back 30-homer, 30-steal seasons. The victory put the

Braves back on top by a half game.

In the second game Charlie Leibrandt hooked up in a pitcher's duel with Orel Hershiser. Justice knocked in a run in the fourth, but the Dodgers tied it in the eighth and won it in the ninth, getting the winning tally off reliever Mike Stanton. That put the Dodgers back on top. Then came the rubber game, Glavine going for his 20th win against Ramon Martinez of the Dodgers.

Glavine had been having first-inning problems in a number of his starts and this one was no exception. L.A. got a pair in the first and then one more in the fourth, knocking out the Atlanta southpaw. Martinez made it stand up, the Dodgers taking a 3–0 victory and a game-and-a-half lead in the standings. The Dodgers had 11 games remaining, the Braves 12. Many now believed L.A. was in the driver's seat.

The next week was a standoff. Atlanta gained a half game by virtue of playing one extra contest. Going into the final week of the season, the Dodgers were 90–66, the Braves 89–67. Atlanta made several personnel moves, picking up veteran pitcher Mike Bielecki and catcher Damon Berryhill from the Cubs for some minor-leaguers. Neither player would be eligible for postseason, but maybe they could help win a game or two.

The Braves did something else as well. They activated Deion Sanders on a per-game basis.

Sanders would be in uniform when he could get leave from his duties with the Falcons. He would be used primarily as a pinch runner, but he set a precedent of sorts. He was the first pro athlete in history to play two sports simultaneously.

A player who had contributed even more, however, was Alejandro Pena. He had become an indispensable closer for Manager Cox. Since giving up two runs in his first appearance for Atlanta, Pena had been perfect in his last 13⅔ innings. He had a 2–0 record with the Braves and hadn't blown a save in seven opportunities.

It was one of the great divisional races of recent years. The two teams were neck and neck and each game was big! On Monday, the Dodgers beat San Diego and Smoltz shut out Cincinnati, 4–0, to even his record at 13–13. The next day the Dodgers won again, but the Braves kept pace with a heart-stopping 7–6 victory over the Reds.

In this one, the Reds erupted for six runs in the first off Leibrandt, but the Braves clawed back. They got two in the fourth, one in the fifth and two in the seventh to pull within a run. Then in the ninth, facing the usually overpowering Rob Dibble, David Justice belted a clutch, two-run homer to give Atlanta the lead. Pena came on to get his 13th save and the Braves had won again, remaining a game behind L.A.

On Wednesday things got about as tight as

they could get. The Dodgers were beaten by San Diego, while the Braves whipped Cincinnati again, 6–3, as Glavine won his 20th. Going into the final weekend of the season, the two teams were dead even. The Braves would be playing lowly Houston, while the Dodgers had three against arch-rival San Francisco. The schedule finally favored the Braves.

In the Friday game, the Braves jumped on top of the Astros quickly, building a 4–0 lead and then coasting home behind Steve Avery, who won his 18th with ninth-inning help from Pena, who got his 15th save. At San Francisco, the Dodgers were crumbling. The Giants got three runs off Ramon Martinez in the first, then coasted to a 4–1 victory behind the pitching of Bud Black. The Braves had the lead by one game with two left.

On Saturday, Atlanta made history. John Smoltz continued his remarkable comeback by whipping the Astros, 5–2, in a route-going performance. The win raised his record to 14–13 and his second-half mark to 12–2. He had pitched as well as any hurler in the league. But that was only half of it. In San Francisco, south-paw Trevor Wilson was handcuffing the Dodgers, spinning a two-hit shutout as the Giants won, 4–0. The race was over. The Braves had done it. They had won a division title. They had gone from worst to first.

FROM WORST TO FIRST!

A Dodger win and Braves loss the final day were meaningless. Atlanta finished at 94–68 to win it by one game. The Braves had been incredible under pressure, winning eight straight games until the meaningless loss at the end. Like any great championship team, they had simply taken the bull by the horns.

But there was even more significance to the victory. The city of Atlanta had not had a champion of any kind in 81 professional sports seasons, taking in its baseball, football, basketball and hockey teams.

"It was a glamour team against a Cinderella team and it was incredible," said team president Stan Kasten. "This was a race people will talk about for years to come."

The people of Atlanta certainly would. They had taken this team of scrappers and fighters to heart. They filled Atlanta-Fulton County Stadium swinging their foam tomahawks (the symbol of the Braves) in unison in a motion that had become known as the Tomahawk Chop. They cheered, chanted and rooted their team home.

Some of the Dodgers groused about the Braves' opponents going soft, even tanking games so that L.A. would lose. The Braves didn't answer. They just played ball.

"There was very little pressure in our clubhouse," said Greg Olson. "There should have been, but there wasn't."

FROM WORST TO FIRST!

Manager Cox also knew his team had just gone out and played. "We weren't destined and all that," he said. "We have very good talent, a very good team."

Pittsburgh Pirates manager Jim Leyland, whose team would meet the Braves in the play-offs, also showed respect for these upstart players from the South. "It didn't take a rocket scientist to realize the Braves were a much better team this year," Leyland said. "I knew they were for real early in the season. You could see it, you could feel it when you played them. There was a new enthusiasm and the young players were really coming along."

A number of the individual performances were outstanding. Pendleton was the National League batting champ with a .319 mark. He also had a career-best 22 homers and drove home 86 runs, making him an MVP candidate. Justice returned from his injury to finish with 21 homers and 87 RBI's in just 396 at bats. Gant had 32 dingers and a team-best 105 ribbies.

And there were others. Treadway hit .320. Blauser had 11 homers and 54 ribbies. Young Brian Hunter had 12 homers and drove home 50. On and on. Everyone came through.

The four starters were all outstanding. Glavine was 20–11, Avery 18–8, Leibrandt 15–11, Smoltz 14–13 with that great second half. Pena wound up with 15 saves (11 for 11 and a 1.40

ERA with the Braves), Stanton 7 and Mercker 6.

There was a newfound respect for the Braves everywhere. One vanquished opponent, Brett Butler of the Dodgers, probably summed it up best when he said, "We didn't lose the West in this last week. We lost it after the All-Star break. Give credit to Atlanta for winning fifty-five games since then. They took it from us."

The Braves had bucked the odds, persevered and gone from last to first. The question now was, could the Cinderella season continue? As Jeff Blauser said, nothing was impossible.

"At the beginning of the year, Las Vegas would have made the odds five hundred to one against us," he said. "That's why this is the world's greatest game. It's not like this in other sports. I don't want to get too philosophical, but baseball is the epitome of America. We were down and out, but we battled back. And now, we're here."

The Twins

There was no need for the Twins to make the kind of stretch run the Braves were forced to make. Minnesota had a solid lead going into

September and simply kept it. Neither the White Sox nor the A's could really mount a challenge, go on an extended winning streak or significantly close the gap. Nor did the Twins crumble. They continued to play the same outstanding baseball they had been playing for most of the season.

The only continuing concern was the condition of the pitching staff. Since the All-Star break the starters had a collective 4.57 ERA, and that wasn't so hot. But the good news was that Erickson had won two straight, raising his record to 18–6. Still, his ERA was up to 3.13 on the season, a far cry from his first-half performance. Tapani, on the other hand, was now 14–7 with a 2.82 ERA. He was 12–1 since his 2–6 start. Many felt he had been the club's best pitcher in the second half. Morris was Morris, a 16–10 pitcher who had the experience needed in the big game.

Aguilera was having a brilliant season as a closer. He now had 38 saves, a career high, and over the past month was 2–0 with 8 saves and an 0.75 ERA. He had gotten great setup support from young Carl Willis, who was 8–3 with 2 saves in just 31 games.

By September 15, the Twins still had a seven and a half game lead over the White Sox. Barring a complete collapse, they seemed to be in great shape to complete a worst-to-first run. But none of the players was taking anything for granted, a good sign. As utility man Al Newman said, "I don't think we've got what you'd call a comfortable lead. I'm still worried about it. I always worry. We've got six games with Chicago and six with Toronto. That's twelve games with some pretty good teams. You don't know what's going to happen."

The hitting continued to hold up. Puckett was at .326 with 80 RBI's. Shane Mack was having a great second half, hitting .312 with 18 homers and 72 ribbies. Designated hitter Davis was up to 28 dingers and 88 RBI's, while Hrbek had 17 and 81. So there was plenty of firepower going into the final weeks of the season.

By the time the Twins reached the 150-game mark they were still eight games in front. They also had a fine 90–60 record. Once again they survived a slight slump. They lost six of eight, allowing the White Sox to get within six games of the lead. But when Chicago lost two of three to the Angels on the weekend, the lead went back to a more comfortable eight games. Defending champ Oakland was 11½ out. The A's were cooked, their three-year run at the top over.

Finally, on September 29, the Twins made history. Though they lost that day to Toronto, 2–1, the White Sox were bowing at Seattle, giving Minnesota the A.L. West title and making them the first team ever to go from worst to first.

The club clinched with seven games left, becoming the second team after Pittsburgh in the National League East to wrap up a divisional crown.

They didn't totally back in. The day before, Jack Morris had pitched a nifty six-hit shutout over the Blue Jays to run his record to 18–12. Earlier in the week Erickson had pitched a strong game, going seven innings and allowing just one hit and a pair of runs in a 9–2 win over the White Sox. That put his record at 19–7. So the club was gearing up for the playoffs.

Twins general manager Andy MacPhail believed the 1991 Minnesota club was even stronger than the '87 team which had won the World Series. MacPhail described that team as "the little engine that could." But he called the current team an express locomotive.

"Despite our 1990 finish and the high level of competition in our division, we left spring training believing we were significantly improved and going to be in the mix all the way," he said. "To do what we have done in the most extraordinarily competitive division in the history of baseball is one heck of an accomplishment.

"If you expected a team to be up by eight games with ten to play, you would have expected it to be Oakland, not us. To win it like we have is a credit to Kelly and the players."

Designated hitter Chili Davis thought the diversity of the Minnesota lineup was what made them so effective. "It's impossible to pitch us just one way," he said. "We have a super-aggressive hitter in Puckett, a patient guy in myself, a power guy like Hrbek, line drive guys like Knoblauch and Harper. And the sky's the limit for Shane Mack."

A number of the Twins raved about their manager. Tom Kelly was a clever handler of players and well respected by everyone.

"I've played for TK since instructional ball and he hasn't changed one bit," said Kirby Puckett. "His door is always open. You can talk to him about anything, baseball or personal. Some managers say that, but you don't believe it. You figure if you speak your mind, you'll get in trouble. TK treats you up front and honest."

Catcher Brian Harper put it this way: "TK prepares a team for each game better than any manager I have ever played for."

The Twins finished the season in Toronto, dropping two of three. Ironically, they would remain there to begin the playoffs against the Eastern Division-winning Blue Jays. They started second-line hurlers in the two games they lost, but in the middle game of the set Erickson pitched six scoreless innings to earn his 20th victory of the season.

There was little doubt about a great team effort. Puckett, Brian Harper, Mack and utility man Randy Bush all hit over .300. Davis led in homers and RBI's (29 and 93), but both Puckett and Hrbek drove in 89 and Mack had 74. Rookie Scott Leius and part-timer Gene Larkin each hit .286, while Hrbek was at .284 and rookie Knoblauch at .281.

Erickson wound up at 20–8, while Morris was 18–12 and Tapani 16–9. They were a formidable Big Three, with Aguilera backing them up with his 42 saves. Willis, Terry Leach, Bedrosian, Mark Guthrie and David West gave the club a sound supporting mound staff. There was little doubt the Twins were ready for the playoffs. When someone mentioned that the Blue Jays had beaten the Twins in all four series during the year, two games to one in each, Manager Kelly just shrugged. "Showtime doesn't start until Tuesday," he said.

Showtime, the playoffs, the postseason. Whatever they chose to call it, the Twins would be ready. Any team that could go from worst to first wasn't about to quit now.

Chapter Nine

The Playoffs

Before 1969, there were no playoffs. There was simply a pennant winner in each league, with the two teams proceeding directly to the World Series. There was only a playoff in the event two teams were tied at the end of the regular season. But with the advent of divisional play in '69, the playoffs became an integral part of the postseason, with teams from each division battling for the flag and the right to move on to the Series.

Until 1985, the playoffs were a best-of-five series. But beginning that year it was increased to a best-of-seven affair, the same as the World Series. Now, with a worst-to-first team competing in each playoff, the fans' interest was mounting. Could the upstart Atlanta Braves overcome the Pittsburgh Pirates, an outstanding team with a solid blend of pitching and hitting? And could the Twins take the measure of the Blue Jays, a team that had dominated them during the regular season? It wouldn't take long to find the answers.

Braves versus Pirates

Still riding on the cloud nine of a divisional title, the Braves prepared to meet the Pittsburgh Pirates in the National League playoffs. In the Pirates, the Braves would be meeting the team with the best record in baseball. Pittsburgh had won the National League East with a 98–64 mark, finishing a full 14 games ahead of runner-up St. Louis. The Bucs' march to the title was basically unobstructed.

This was a solid Pirates team, managed by Jim Leyland and featuring a number of outstanding players. Outfielder Barry Bonds had been the National League's Most Valuable Player in 1990 and had a second straight great year. Bonds finished with 25 homers, 116 RBI's, a .292 average and 43 stolen bases. Giving him more than able support was the competitive Bobby Bonilla, who hit .302, belting 18 homers, and drove home 100 runs.

Center fielder Andy Van Slyke smacked 17 dingers and drove home 83, while shortstop Jay

Bell had 16 homers and 67 ribbies. The supporting cast was also solid.

On the mound, the Pirates had a Big Three of their own. Lefty John Smiley finished at 20–8, while another southpaw, Zane Smith, was 16–10. Righty Doug Drabek, the Cy Young Award winner in 1990, overcame a horrible start to finish at 15–14 and was probably the club's best big-game pitcher. Bill Landrum and Stan Belinder shared the closer role and had 17 and 16 saves, respectively.

Besides having a fine team, the Pirates also had something to prove. They had been highly favored in the 1990 playoffs and were beaten in six games by Cincinnati. In that series, the vaunted middle of the Bucs lineup—Bonds, Bonilla and Van Slyke—failed to produce the numbers. They didn't want that to happen again.

In addition, it was pointed out that the Braves had beaten the Pirates in 9 of their 12 regular-season meetings. They had dominated. To Manager Cox, that didn't really mean much. "It's all out the window," he said. "That's nothing now."

But the Braves' players thought differently. Catcher Olson said, "It means something mentally. They're supposed to be the best team in baseball, but we had more wins on them than they had on us." Steve Avery added, "What we are doing has worked pretty well against them."

The Pirates, however, were also confident. Bucs catcher Mike LaValliere said pitching would be the difference. "Our pitchers will shut down whoever we play," he said. "That's the key in the postseason. If you have good pitching, you have a good chance to win it."

Tom Glavine was on the mound for the Braves against Doug Drabek as the playoffs opened at Three Rivers Stadium in Pittsburgh before 57,347 fans. As had been his problem in recent months, Glavine struggled in early innings. Van Slyke homered in the first, then doubled in a second run in the third. When Bonilla drove home Van Slyke with a single, the Pirates had a 3–0 lead.

Drabek, in the meantime, was again showing his Cy Young form from the year before. He had blanked the Braves on just three hits through the first six innings. Then, in the bottom of the sixth, Pittsburgh got to Glavine again with Drabek right in the middle of it.

With two out, Drabek connected with a Glavine offering and drove one over Ron Gant's head in center. With a 4–0 lead, the Pirate hurler should have settled for an easy double. Instead, he steamed around second and rambled toward third. The throw nipped the sliding Drabek for the third out. But that wasn't the only out. Drabek's foolish gamble resulted in a pulled hamstring. He had to leave the game. Bob Walk finished up, completing the 5–1 victory. But Drabek was now doubtful for his next start.

"I was mad that I made that decision, especially with two outs and being on second," said Drabek. "Someone gets a hit and I still have a chance to score. But sometimes I make split-second decisions, and once I make 'em, I get a little hardheaded about it and keep on going."

Down a game, the Braves turned to young Steve Avery to try to get them even. Pittsburgh went with southpaw Zane Smith. Smith was very good, but the 6–4, 190-pound Avery dominated. With his fastball reaching a high of 98 mph, the youngster hung the Bucs out to dry. Even the powerful middle of the Pirate order looked helpless against Avery's offerings.

Smith was almost as good. He faltered briefly in the sixth, and the Braves got a run when little-used second sacker Mark Lemke swatted a bad-hop double that drove home David Justice. After that, it was all Avery. He began tiring in the ninth and Pena came on to get the final out. But the 1–0 verdict (a six-hitter with nine strikeouts) had drawn the Braves even and now they were headed home to Atlanta. And people couldn't say enough about Steve Avery. "I had said he'd be toying with hitters by 1993," said Manager Cox. "It looks like I was two years off."

Pirate catcher Don Slaught said Avery had produced "the best pitching performance we've seen all year." "People say Avery has great poise," Pirate manager Leyland commented. "But when you have the kind of stuff he does, it's easy to have great poise."

As for Avery, he was like a kid with a new toy. "I was just having fun out there," he said. "How can you not enjoy it when millions of people are watching and all the attention is on you? It helps me concentrate."

Now the Pirates would have to concentrate in Atlanta, where more than 50,000 fans would be chanting and doing the Tomahawk Chop. And the Braves had their hot pitcher, John Smoltz, taking to the mound against 20-game winner John Smiley. For a few minutes, it looked as if the Pirates might be doing some chopping of their own.

Rookie Orlando Merced led off against Smoltz and took his first pitch downtown. The home run made it 1–0 and when shortstop Jay Bell followed with a single it looked as if Smoltz might be on the ropes. After all, the next three hitters were named Van Slyke, Bonilla and Bonds. But Smoltz bore down and got all three without further damage. That, right there, might have been the key to the game.

For in the bottom of the first the Braves went right to work on Smiley. The Pirate lefty got the first two hitters, then the roof fell in. Gant, Justice and Hunter whacked consecutive doubles, accounting for two runs. Next came catcher Olson, who promptly deposited a Smiley offering in the left field seats for a two-run homer. Before you could say Atlanta-Fulton County Stadium, the Braves had a 4–1 lead.

In the second, Smiley hit Lonnie Smith with a pitch after two were out. Smith took third after he was picked off first, and first sacker Merced threw the ball into left field. Terry Pendleton followed with a double and it was a 5–1 game. By the seventh inning it was 7–3. Then the Pirates loaded the sacks with one out in the top of the eighth. Out went Smoltz and in came Pena.

The fastballing right-hander got Merced to foul out, then poured a called third strike past Jay Bell to retire the side. When the game ended, the Pirates had stranded 11 runners and the Braves had a 10–3 victory and a 2–1 lead in the series. Lefty Randy Tomlin got the call for the Bucs in Game 4, with vet Charlie Leibrandt on the hill for Atlanta.

This one was close all the way. The Braves held a 2–1 lead in the fifth when Justice made a poor judgment, throwing from right field to third to try to cut down the speedy Gary Redus after Bell's single. Redus had it beat all the way, but when the throw skipped past Pendleton, Redus got up from his slide and scored the tying run.

FROM WORST TO FIRST!

It stayed that way until the 10th. Reliever Kent Mercker walked a pair of Bucs, setting up a confrontation between pinch hitter Mike LaValliere and reliever Mark Wohlers. LaValliere delivered a sharp single on an 0–2 pitch, driving home the winning run and tying the playoffs once more at two games each.

After the game, Justice wouldn't make excuses for his throw. "I wouldn't have thrown the ball unless I thought I had a good chance," he said. "That's the way I play—aggressive. All this means is we'll have to go back to Pittsburgh and win it there."

But the Braves didn't want to go back down 3–2. That was why the fifth game was so important. Tom Glavine and Zane Smith were the starters in a playoff series that would now be dominated by pitching. This time Glavine didn't have a shaky start, and the game was scoreless through three, Smith also putting the shackles on the Atlanta bats. The Braves botched an opportunity in the second when, with the bases loaded, Glavine didn't see the sign for a suicide squeeze and Brian Hunter was caught in a rundown. Then came the bottom of the fourth.

Justice led off and was safe on an error, taking second on the miscue. Three batters latter, Mark Lemke singled to left and Justice headed home. But after he scored, the Pirates asked for the ball at third, an appeal play. The umpire ruled Justice had missed the bag and was out. The run didn't count.

"I always follow the runner all the way around in case something happens," said Buc shortstop Jay Bell, who noticed that Justice had missed the bag. "There's no doubt in my mind he missed it. I was right behind him."

Justice saw it differently. "My spikes grazed the bag," he said. "I didn't argue the call because I knew they wouldn't change it. But I know I got it. I wouldn't have kept going (to the plate) if I didn't."

But the run was negated and the game continued scoreless—that is, until the next inning. In the Pirate fifth, a walk and singles by Don Slaught and Jose Lind brought home the first and only run of the ballgame. Smith pitched seven and two-thirds innings and Roger Mason finished up, quelling an Atlanta rally in the ninth to preserve the win. The 1–0 victory put the Bucs up by one. Now the Braves faced the unenviable task of winning twice in Pittsburgh if they didn't want their quest to end.

The Game 6 pitchers were Steve Avery for the Braves and Doug Drabek for the Pirates. Drabek said his hamstring injury was just about healed, then went out and proved it. Once again, the game evolved into a pitching duel, the outcome in doubt until the very last inning.

It was hard to believe that Avery was dominating the Pirates again, but he looked every bit as strong as he had in the second game. He was blowing smoke past the Buc batters. Drabek, on the other hand, was looking just as sharp, setting up his fastball with a variety of curves and off-speed pitches. He wasn't as overpowering as Avery, but he was just as effective.

At the end of eight innings, the game was still scoreless. Avery had given up just three hits, Drabek six. Avery had also fanned eight, one less than in Game 2. Now, in the top of the ninth, the Braves tried to get something going. They knew if it went scoreless into the bottom of the frame they would be facing sudden-death elimination.

Justice led off the Atlanta ninth by grounding out to first. But then the speedy Gant drew a walk. After Bream flied to left for the second out, Gant took off and stole second. Now catcher Olson was up. Drabek was still out there and tried to work Olson carefully. But the Braves catcher slammed a double down the left field line as Gant scampered home with what would be the only run of the game.

Pena came on and promptly gave up a single to Gary Varsho. Merced bunted him over to second. After Bell flied to right, Pena wild-pitched Varsho to third. Now the dangerous Van Slyke was at the plate. After fouling off four Pena fastballs, Van Slyke was frozen by the first change-up Pena had thrown in the series. Strike three! The Braves had won it, 1–0, to send the series to a seventh and deciding game.

"I can't imagine a playoff series being much better than this," said Jim Leyland. "There has been great pitching and great defense, a little bit of everything."

For Greg Olson, getting the game-winning hit was the thrill of a lifetime. "I didn't feel myself touch first base," he said. "I was floating to second. It's going to be tough to go to sleep tonight. If I'm a fan, I want to see seven games, and we've given the fans some great games. They've been exciting to play in, but I'm mentally drained. I don't know how much more I have left."

Even Atlanta general manager John Schuerholz was nearly overwhelmed by the drama of the series. "I wanted a seventh game," he said. "I was watching, doing my deep-breathing exercises, I was in prayerful concentration, anything I thought could work. This is about as good as it could be."

So there was one game left for all the marbles. The Braves had John Smoltz ready to go, while the Pirates would counter with John Smiley, who had been so ineffective in Game 2. The Braves wanted to get to him early again. Sure enough, they did. Gant drove in the first run with a long, sacrifice fly. Two batters later, Brian Hunter belted a two-run homer to make it 3–0.

When Olson followed with a single, Smiley was gone . . . and for all intents and purposes, so were the Pirates.

The Braves got another run on a Hunter double in the fifth, and that was all Smoltz and the Braves needed. The young right-hander went the distance, blanking the Bucs on six hits while fanning eight and pitching the Braves to a 4—0 victory and the National League pennant. The team that had gone from worst to first was now headed for the World Series.

Twins versus Blue Jays

The Toronto Blue Jays had won the American League East by seven games over Boston and Detroit. At 91—71, the Jays had the poorest record of the four divisional champs. The consensus was that the Twins would win and continue to the World Series. But the Jays also had something to prove, especially since blowing a 3—1 lead to the Kansas City Royals in the 1985 ALCS playoffs.

This wasn't a bad Blue Jays team, though it didn't have a single .300 hitter or 20-game winner. Joe Carter was the top slugger with 33 homers and 108 RBI's. Roberto Alomar, Devon White, Kelly Gruber and John Olerud could also handle the stick. Jimmy Key was the top pitcher with a 16–12 slate, while David Wells and Todd Stottlemyre won 15 each. Duane Ward and Tom Henke had 55 saves between them. Rookie Juan Guzman also gave the team a 10–3 lift after a midseason call-up.

The Twins, however, felt they were ready. The players were confident they could handle the Jays. They were also glad that veteran Jack Morris was ready for the opener. Morris was one guy who wouldn't rattle. He had been there before, with the Tigers back in 1984. That year he won a game in the playoffs and two more in the World Series.

Tom Candiotti, a knuckleballer who had come over from Cleveland, was the Toronto starter in the opener, played at the Metrodome. As always, the boisterous Twins fans were out in droves, shouting encouragement to their heroes and waving their omnipresent white homer hankies. Maybe the entire atmosphere unnerved Candiotti and the Jays, because the Twins wasted no time in striking.

Part of the problem was that Candiotti's knuckler was really dancing. The righty threw 60 pitches in two and a half innings of work and the Twins made contact on 23 of the 31 pitches they went after. They also swiped four bases during that time and quickly built up a 5–0 lead. Morris wasn't super-sharp, either. He gave up a run in the fourth, then was touched for three more in the sixth before he gave way to Carl Willis. That brought the score to 5–4, but Willis and Rick Aguilera shut the door without further damage. Minnesota had broken on top.

Game 2, however, was a different story. The Blue Jays went with the rookie, Juan Guzman, while Minnesota countered with Kevin Tapani. This time it was Tapani who didn't have his good stuff. Toronto jumped on him for three runs in the first three innings, taking a 3–1 lead. The Twins narrowed it to 3–2 in the sixth, but another pair off Tapani and reliever Steve Bedrosian in the seventh put things on ice. The final was 5–2, marking the Twins' first postseason loss in the Metrodome in seven postseason games.

Now it was back to the Sky Dome in Toronto, a stadium that had produced record crowds the past two years. The Jays felt pretty good because they had split in Minneapolis and now were home. They had their top winner ready in Jimmy Key. The Twins, however, had 20-game winner Scott Erickson set to take the hill, hoping he would regain his early-season form.

In the very first inning, however, it was apparent that Erickson wasn't on his game. He was overthrowing his fastball and rushing his pitches. That meant the Twins were in trouble. They paid the price when Joe Carter slammed a solo homer, followed by a walk to Olerud, an infield single by Gruber and a run-scoring double by Candy Maldonado. It was a 2–0 after one.

"Damn right I was worried," Manager Kelly admitted afterward. "If you get behind two-zip and your kid pitcher throws the ball thirty-one times in the first inning and you're trying to get through a best-of-seven series with just three starters like we are, then you'd be worried, too."

Erickson settled down somewhat after that and pitched into the fifth inning. The Twins had just gotten one back in the top of the inning when Mack tripled and scored on Hrbek's fielder's choice grounder. Erickson walked Alomar to start the home half of the frame. Then, with a 1–2 count on Carter, Manager Kelly suddenly replaced his starter with David West.

"Scott was plain whacked out," said Kelly. "Carter had just hit a couple of rockets off him, though both were foul. The kid was just too nervous and the pressure finally wore him out."

West pitched out of the inning, and in the sixth the Twins tied it. Rookie Knoblauch ripped a double, followed by a single to right by Puckett. There was a close play at the plate, but Knoblauch got in under the tag. Then the relievers took over, neither team able to score. It was still tied after nine and as the Twins came up in the top of the 10th, righty Mike Timlin was on the mound for the Blue Jays.

Timlin got Gene Larkin to ground to second. Then Mike Pagliarulo came up to bat for Scott Leius. Pags, the former Yankee, went after a 1–0 pitch and drove the ball deep into the right field seats for a home run, giving the Twins a 3–2 lead. Rick Aguilera came out of the pen to retire the Jays in 1-2-3 fashion in the bottom of the inning. The Twins had won it and had taken a 2–1 lead.

"A lot of people thought Pags was washed up," said Kirby Puckett after the game. "But we knew he could play."

"I wasn't begging for a job," said the happy Pagliarulo. "There were a couple of other teams interested. But I knew I needed a situation that was right for me. That's why I signed with the Twins."

Now Pags had paid a major dividend. He had put his team back in the league with one swing of the bat. As he joked to reporters, "It was the shortest game of my life, but it was my best game."

So Game 4 suddenly began a "must" contest for the Jays. Young Todd Stottlemyre was Manager Cito Gaston's choice to throw, while the Twins calmly returned to the veteran Jack Morris, even though the 36-year-old hurler was coming back on three days' rest. Dan Gladden, the

Twin's left fielder, admitted the rest of the team had a special feeling when Morris was on the hill.

"Everyone enjoys playing behind Jack," said Gladden. "It seems like we give a bit extra for him because we know he's busting his butt, too. His reputation speaks for itself. He's a competitor and for some reason we seem to pick up the level behind him."

They picked it up in Game 4, all right. Toronto took a 1–0 lead in the second on a single by Maldonado, a wild pitch and base hit by Pat Borders. But in the fourth, the Twins took over. Puckett started it with a long homer to center field. Later in the inning Pagliarulo singled home another run, then Gladden singled in two more. That got rid of Stottlemyre and gave the Twins a 4–1 lead.

Minnesota got two more in the sixth, Pags and Gladden getting the RBI's once again. After that, the Twins just pecked away, finally winning it 9–3. Morris went the first eight to get his second victory of the playoffs and give his club a commanding 3–1 lead. He came up big when he had to and was pleased with his performance.

"My fastball was good enough," he said. "I didn't throw a change-up, but basically I had command of my pitches all night."

Now the Twins were going for the kill. They would like nothing better than to clinch in To-

ronto, then go home and await the winner of the
Pittsburgh-Atlanta series in the National League.
Kevin Tapani was back on the mound against
Tom Candiotti. This would be a wild and woolly
game, but a game that showed the mettle of the
Minnesota Twins and stamped them as an out-
standing baseball team.

In a game of ebb and flow, the Twins took
charge first. Puckett belted a solo homer in the
opening frame, and Shane Mack drove in another run with a single in the second. But the
2–0 lead only lasted an inning. In the third, the
Jays got to Tapani, four hits driving in three
runs. Now Toronto had the lead, 3–2.

The Jays built it to 5–2 in the fourth, getting
three more hits and a pair of runs off Tapani.
David West took over in the fifth. Then in the
top of the sixth Minnesota rallied again. Mack
and Pagliarulo singled. Randy Tomlin relieved
Candiotti. After a foul out, one run came in on
a fielder's choice and the tying runs scored on
a clutch double by Knoblauch.

It stayed tied until the Minnesota eighth. Facing Duane Ward, Greg Gagne singled with one
out, but was caught stealing. Gladden than
slapped a two-out single and Knoblauch followed with a walk. Up came Puckett, facing lefty
David Wells. The compact but powerful center
fielder then rapped a double, scoring Gladden

and sending Knoblauch to third. The Twins had the lead at 6–5.

Moments later Ken Hrbek dealt Toronto the coup de grace. He singled to drive home a pair of insurance runs and make the score 8–5. Carl Willis retired the Jays in the eighth, helped by a slick 5–6–3 double play. And in the ninth it was the closer Aguilera, setting the Jays down in order, ending their season and making the Twins worst-to-first American League champions. They also became the first team ever to win three games on the road in a championship series.

Kirby Puckett was the ALCS Most Valuable Player, going 7-for-16 for the series and getting six of the hits in the final two games.

"A lot of guys wrote Kirby off after he went one-for-seven in the first two games," said Tom Kelly. "But he had a good three games here. He can get ten hits faster than anyone I've ever seen."

As was his way, Puckett was more interested in talking about the team than about himself. "Even when we lost last year, this team had a lot of dignity," he said. "We weren't the Bad News Bears or anything. And I'm not going to lie to you and say I thought we would win the American League pennant and go to the World Series. No, I just knew that we wouldn't finish last again."

FROM WORST TO FIRST!

That they wouldn't finish last again became obvious very early in the season. That they would win their division became obvious fairly soon after the All-Star break. They they would win the playoff became pretty obvious after Games 3 and 4. Now there was one more stop, one more hurdle to clear to make their worst-to-first odyssey a real fairy tale.

But if the story had a once-upon-a-time beginning, it would have a storybook ending either way. Both teams about to play the fall classic would have a chance to make history, because both the Twins and their adversaries, the Braves, had now done the same thing. They had come from the bottom and landed on the top. Now they would be saying hello to each other from opposite sides of the diamond.

Chapter Ten

The World Series

Even before it started people were saying it was too bad there would have to be a loser. Both the Braves and the Twins were modern-day Cinderella teams, captivating the baseball world at large with their amazing one-season turnarounds. Each club took its own road to a division title, then showed grit, desire and determination in winning its respective playoff series. As the ballclubs gathered at the Metrodome in Minnesota to begin the World Series, they both believed their seasons were too storied already not to go the rest of the way.

The Braves were well aware of what happened the last time the Twins had been in the World Series. Minnesota had opened the 1987 classic with a pair of wins at the Metrodome. Then the Twins traveled to St. Louis, where they lost three straight. But back home again, they won the final two games to become world champs, and also to become the first team in Series history to win all four games at home.

One thing the Braves were wary of was the tremendous noise level at the Metrodome. It had become almost legendary after the '87 Series. Even Kirby Puckett admitted that he "had a headache for two weeks after the eighty-seven Series because of all the crowd noise."

Terry Pendleton was a member of the '87 Cardinal team. "I tried to wear earplugs at the Dome," he recalled, "but I couldn't keep them in because they made me feel like I was under water."

Catcher Mike Heath, unable to play for the Braves because of an injury, also recalled many trips to the Metrodome when he was with the Detroit Tigers. "Sometimes, you just can't hear your teammates over that din," he said. "On any throws from the outfield, the first baseman and third baseman really have to take charge. They're going to have to cut off throws on instinct because nobody can hear the catcher yelling 'cut.' They'll have to develop hand signals."

One person who didn't think the noise level would be a factor the way it had been in '87 was the Twins' Kent Hrbek. "I live here all year, so it's easy for me to notice that the fans haven't been as excited this year as they were in eighty-seven," Hrbek said. "In 1987, the decibel levels were recorded at one hundred twenty-five, which is louder than a jet airplane engine. I'm told the decibel level never got over one hundred eighteen so far this year."

There were a couple of other things about the Metrodome that had the Braves' attention, if not their concern.

"What was the architect who designed this place thinking about?" asked Braves' center fielder Ron Gant. "Why would you want to put a white roof on a place when the players have to look up at it when they try to follow a white baseball?"

And Manager Cox addressed still another problem. "The artificial surface is as hard as concrete," he said. "It's faster than anything in the National League. That means hard-hit ground balls can go all the way to the fence if your outfielders can't cut them off. Second, the banks of lights are lower than in outdoor stadiums, which means there are certain areas of the playing surface where your fielders can be blinded if the ball is hit on a low trajectory."

It almost sounded as if the Metrodome was an extra player, a superstar who could turn the Series around without hitting, catching or throwing. But the Braves were professionals. Once the action started, the players would concentrate to the point where the Dome wouldn't bother them. Or would it?

On the other hand, the Braves had themselves a good-luck charm. Outfielder Lonnie Smith was playing in his fourth World Series with his fourth team. The other three had all emerged winners—the 1980 Phillies, 1982 Cardinals and 1985 Royals. Smith and the Braves were hoping the magic would work once again.

Also, for the game in Minnesota, both teams would be allowed to use the designated hitter. But when the Series swung back to Atlanta, the pitchers would have to hit. That too could be an advantage for the Braves, since American League hurlers never have to face living pitching during the regular season or in the playoffs. In addition, the Twins had an outstanding DH in Chili Davis. Unless Manager Kelly wanted to risk Davis's shaky glove in the outfield, the Twins would lose his power bat in Atlanta.

It came as no surprise when Manager Kelly named Jack Morris to pitch the opener for the Twins. He had been the big-game guy all year and by starting Game 1 he would be available for three starts if it went the distance. The surprise was the Braves' starter. It would be veteran lefty Charlie Leibrandt. Manager Cox figured that Leibrandt was a logical choice because he had pitched in the Metrodome from his days with the Kansas City Royals. He was less likely to be rattled by the crowd noise. That way, the young pitchers could get used to the noise and get an extra day of rest at the same time.

"Using Charlie isn't ever a give-up, not by any

means," Cox said. "I'm also serious about using him in a fifth game and if I do make a change in the rotation it won't come until the morning of that fifth game."

There were 55,108 fans at the Metrodome, most of them waving the homer hankies and cheering, though the noise didn't seem to reach quite the level it had in 1987. Both pitchers tossed goose eggs for the first two innings. Morris, as usual, was responding to the pressure, but Leibrandt also looked solid. Then in the third the Twins made the first breakthrough.

After Scott Leius grounded out and Greg Gagne fanned, Dan Gladden drew a walk. With rookie Chuck Knoblauch at the plate, Gladden swiped second. Knoblauch then came through with a base hit to right, scoring Gladden with the first run of the Series. When Knoblauch tried to stretch to a double, he was cut down on a brisk relay from Justice to first sacker Bream to shortstop Belliard. But the Twins had drawn first blood.

Then in the fifth they KO'd Leibrandt. Hrbek started it off with a double to right. Leius singled him to third. Now shortstop Gagne was up. He had hit just eight homers during the regular season, but that didn't matter now. The 0–1 pitch from Leibrandt was right there and Gagne jerked it into the left field seats for a three-run homer.

That made the score 4–0 and sent Leibrant to the showers.

The Braves got one back on a Ron Gant single in the sixth, but Minneapolis came right back when Hrbek blasted a solo homer in the bottom of the inning. That made it 5–1. In the Atlanta eighth, Morris walked the first two hitters and was replaced by Mark Guthrie, who got Pendleton to hit into a double play. But after a walk to Justice, Aguilera came in. Gant singled to drive in the second Braves run, but after that Aggie closed the door. He also retired the Braves in the ninth, and the Twins had won the opener, 5–2.

One of the happiest Twins was first baseman Hrbek, who had been slumping throughout the playoffs. He had broken out with two hits, including a homer.

"I've failed before," Hrbek said. "In fact, I've failed a bunch. Everyone in this room has failed. But that's what makes a major-leaguer. There are guys in the minors who fail and never make it. But I take it all in stride and I know I'm swinging the bat better."

So the Twins had won once again in the Dome. That made the second game more important. The Braves would love to come away with a split. Now they had 20-game winner Tom Glavine on the hill against the Twins' Kevin Tapani. Glavine was known for his first-inning problems and the Twins were well aware that his first-inning ERA was over 10.00. They also knew he was just 3–3 with a 4.22 ERA in his final seven regular season starts.

After Tapani retired the Braves in the top of the first, the Twins went to work. Gladden reached second on a fielding error by right fielder Justice. Then Knoblauch walked. Puckett was next, but Glavine got him to bounce into a double play that erased Gladden at third. With Knoblauch on second, designated hitter Davis blasted a Glavine pitch into the left field seats and the Twins were on top again, 2–0.

To Glavine's credit, he didn't rattle. The southpaw settled down and began handling the Minnesota hitters. In the top of the second the Braves got one back. After Justice singled to center, Bream whacked a double down the left field line, Justice stopping at third. Brian Hunter then hit a sacrifice fly to right, scoring Justice. But Tapani toughened and got Olson on a groundout and Lemke on a called third strike.

In the Atlanta third came the first controversial play of the Series. After Belliard grounded out, designated hitter Smith was safe on an error. Tapani then got Pendleton on a fly to center. But when Gant singled, Smith motored to third. Gant took a big turn at first and when Tapani cut off the throw from the outfield, he fired to Hrbek at first.

Gant appeared to get back in time, but his leg tangled with Hrbek's. The 250-pound first sacker literally lifted Gant off the bag and applied the tag. Gant was called out and went into a rage. Most observers also thought he'd been forced off the bag and that it was a bad call. But it stuck and the rally was killed.

"The players are going to do whatever they can to try to get a call," Gant said later. "That's why we have umpires out there. I can't blame Hrbek for doing that. I probably would have tried the same thing. But it was so obvious what happened."

It was still a 2–1 game in the fifth and this time the Braves tied it. Olson doubled, went to third on a Lemke groundout and scored on a sacrifice fly by Belliard. It remained a 2–2 game until the bottom of the eighth. Tapani had just pitched out of trouble in the top of the inning, getting Gant and Justice with runners on first and third.

Glavine was still in there for Atlanta, having thrown six scoreless frames since the first. The lead-off hitter was third sacker Scott Leius, who had hit just five homers during the regular season. But when he got a pitch he liked, he promptly put the ball in the left field stands for the go-ahead run. That made it a 3–2 ballgame. Then Aguilera came on to do his thing in the ninth, and it was over. Minnesota had a 2–0 lead as the Series got set to shift to the home of the Tomahawk Chop.

"We can't blame the ballpark or the umpires for this loss," said Manager Cox. "We could have won with a clutch hit, but we didn't get one."

"It was a gutty performance by Tapani," Manager Kelly said, after sticking with his starter through the threat in the eighth.

The third game was a classic. Atlanta had young Steve Avery set to go, hoping he would be the same hot pitcher he'd been in the playoffs. Minnesota countered with Scott Erickson, and the Twins hoped he would exhibit the form he'd shown in the first half, when he'd been the best pitcher in the majors. As it turned out, it was a very long night that before it was over would see 13 pitchers parade to the mound.

In the first inning, the Twins got rid of Avery's aura of invincibility. Gladden opened the game with a triple to right and promptly scored on a sacrifice fly off the bat of Knoblauch. Erickson retired the Braves in the first, but beginning in the second it was obvious the young righty didn't have it.

A walk and two singles gave the Braves their first run. They got another in the fourth when Justice led off with a long homer to right. That made it 2–1. In the fifth, Lonnie Smith homered to make it 3–1. Pendleton then walked. He took second on a wild pitch. When Justice was safe on an error, Pendleton went to third.

David West was brought in to relieve Erickson. He promptly walked Bream and Olson to force in yet another run. Manager Kelly then replaced West with Terry Leach, who got out of the inning. But the Braves had taken a 4–1 lead. It stayed that way until the seventh, when Puckett homered off Avery to make it 4–2.

Then in the Twins' eighth, pinch hitter Brian Harper was safe on an error. Manager Cox removed Avery in favor of Alejandro Pena, his closer. But pinch hitter Chili Davis greeted Pena with a two-run homer that tied the game at 4–4. That's when the parade of players and pitchers started. Both teams blew scoring opportunities and the game went into extra innings.

The Twins rallied in the 12th and Manager Kelly was forced to use Rick Aguilera as a pinch hitter. Aggie had hit well when he was in the National League and was up in a bases-loaded situation. Kelly had to use him because he was almost out of pitchers, and Mark Guthrie, the pitcher who was in the game for Minnesota, had never been at bat in the big leagues. Aguilera, however, hadn't hit since July 20, 1989, when he'd still been with the Mets.

Jim Clancy was on the hill for the Braves, and Aguilera actually hit the ball hard. He slammed a line drive to center that was gloved by Gant for the final out.

"I felt the ball hit my bat and started to run," Aggie said. "I hit it pretty decent. I was hoping Gant was playing a little more shallow than that, but he caught it."

Then in the bottom of the 12th the Braves won it. With one out, Justice singled to right. After Hunter popped out, Justice stole second. Olson then walked and Mark Lemke slapped a single to left, Justice scoring just ahead of the tag by Brian Harper. The Braves had won it, 5—4, to pull within a game of the Twins.

Jack Morris got the ball for the Twins once more in Game 4. He was oppposed by right-hander John Smoltz. Ironically, Smoltz had grown up in Detroit and his early pitching idol was none other than Jack Morris.

"What I remember most about Jack was his competitiveness," said Smoltz, some 12 years Morris's junior. "He went after each batter with one hundred percent no matter what the score was. He battled you on every pitch. That's the way I approach things when I pitch now."

So it was teacher against pupil and both did their thing, going after every hitter as if the entire World Series depended on it. The result was another close, hard-fought baseball game. The Twins scored one in the second; the Braves evened it in the third. Then both pitchers matched goose eggs until the seventh. That's when the Twins took a 2–1 lead. Carl Willis replaced Morris in the bottom of the inning and Atlanta promptly tied it.

It was still a 2–2 game going to the bottom of the ninth. Mark Guthrie started the inning for Minnesota. Mark Lemke, the little guy who was suddenly wielding a big bat, got the key hit, a big triple with one out. Right-hander Steve Bedrosian then came in and Manager Cox sent up journeyman Jerry Willard, a third-string catcher who had been in and out of the majors since 1984.

Another unlikely hero, Willard lofted a fly to medium right. Shane Mack backed up, then caught the ball as he moved forward into throwing position. Lemke tried it. The play was close as catcher Harper lunged at the sliding base runner. Safe! Harper had touched Lemke with his body, but not with the glove and ball. The Braves had won it, 3–2, to even the Series at two games each.

At the safe call, Harper shouted, "No way, I got him! I got him!" Later he admitted his reaction had been emotional. "I really believed I got him. But the umpire said he made contact with my shoulder. I thought I tagged him with my glove."

Harper had already made a pair of dramatic tag plays in the game, in one being bowled over on a vicious collision with Lonnie Smith. But he had held the ball for the out. It was that kind of game.

"Two good games that we've come out on the losing end both times," said Manager Kelly. "Not too good."

But Kirby Puckett indicated he and his teammates weren't panicking. "We're still loose," Puckett said. "Remember, we're not even supposed to be here. Oakland is supposed to be here or Chicago is supposed to be here. Not us."

For Game 5, Manager Cox did make the change he had talked about. He bypassed Charlie Leibrandt and went back to Tom Glavine. Minnesota stuck with its three-man rotation and returned Kevin Tapani to the mound. As it turned out, it probably didn't matter who pitched for the Braves. The Atlanta hitters finally unloaded, making this one the only laugher of the Series.

The Braves exploded for four runs in the fourth inning, six more in the seventh and three in the eighth. The final was 14–5, as Atlanta smacked out 17 hits and scored the most runs in a World Series game in 31 years. David Justice had five RBI's, Mark Lemke smacked out a pair of triples, and Lonnie Smith hit his third home run of the Series and third in three games.

Atlanta had a 5–0 lead with Glavine throwing a three-hitter through five innings. In the sixth, the left-hander suddenly lost the plate. Sixteen of his final 20 pitches were balls, and the final 8 were all off the plate. Fortunately for the Braves, Minnesota got just three runs and in the bottom of the inning the Braves broke it wide open.

Back in the Metrodome for Game 6, the Twins and their fans could only hope that history would repeat itself. In 1987 the Twins had come back to the Dome trailing the Cardinals 3–2. That year they won the final two games to take the Series. Scott Erickson was the Minnesota pitcher, taking the hill against Steve Avery. There was continued concern that Erickson still wasn't throwing hard because of that elbow problem around midseason.

"He just hasn't had the good pop since the elbow problem," said one scout. "He's gotten by some days because his ball moves well, but he's not anything special without that real hard sinking fastball."

Supposedly, the radar gun showed that Erickson was throwing at 82 to 84 mph in Game 3. Early in the season he'd been throwing at 89 to 90 mph.

"I'm not worried about my speed," Erickson said. "I know I could have thrown a couple of pitches faster, but I was happy on my velocity on some other pitches. Maybe because everyone was worried about me pitching too hard I took a little off."

As it turned out, Erickson still wasn't super-sharp, but neither was Avery. The Twins scored first, Puckett tripling in a run in the first, then scoring the second tally on a base hit by Shane Mack. In the third, Puckett stopped an Atlanta rally with a spectacular leaping catch of a Ron Gant drive against the center field fence.

In the fifth, a two-run homer by Pendleton tied the game, but Puckett's sacrifice fly in the bottom of the inning gave the Twins the lead again. The Braves didn't quit, however, tying the game in the seventh and finally getting Erickson out of there. Lemke started it with a single and Manager Kelly promptly brought in left-hander Mark Guthrie.

Guthrie fanned pinch hitter Jeff Blauser, but then a wild pitch and walk to Smith put runners on first and second. Pendleton then beat out a slow roller to fill the bases. Gant was next and hit a slow grounder to deep short. The throw to second got Pendleton, but Gant used his speed to beat a relay throw to first and avoid the double play. Lemke scored and the game was tied at 3–3.

It stayed that way through nine, and once again the two teams had to play extras. It was still the Twins who had their backs to the wall. The Braves had Pena pitch the 9th and 10th, while Kelly went to his stopper, Aguilera. But when the Twins came up to hit in the bottom of the 11th, Pena was gone and Charlie Leibrandt, the guy bumped in Game 5, was on the hill. The batter was Kirby Puckett, the Twins' hottest hitter.

Leibrandt ran the count to 2–1. Then Puckett connected, a long shot to deep left that cleared the fence for a heart-stopping, game-winning home run. The Series was tied again and the Twins were still alive.

"I figured somebody had to step forward," a jubilant Puckett said. "I've been here before. I was ready to let it stand out."

Scott Erickson, who hung tough without his real good stuff, said what all the Twins were thinking: "In big games you have to turn it on, and Kirby's our big-money player."

Braves manager Cox defended his choice of Leibrandt, saying, "Why not Leibrandt? He's faced Puckett before. He keeps the ball down. He's a fifteen-game winner. Charlie just got the ball up and Puckett hit it hard."

Now it was down to a single game. The script couldn't have been any better, a rematch between Jack Morris and John Smoltz. The two worst-to-first teams had battled and battled, and had now taken it to the limit. The veteran Morris, for one, couldn't wait to start the final game.

"Let's get it on," he told reporters. "I don't

know any pitcher who wouldn't look forward to a game like this. I don't feel any pressure, I'm relaxed. I've been in World Series games before and I'm used to big games. It's something I enjoy."

Smoltz too was ready. "This is a situation I've played out a lot in my mind when I was younger," he said. "I'll be like a little kid out there. Naturally, I was hoping that I wouldn't have to do this and we'd win on Saturday. But I look at it as a challenge."

The game turned out to be a classic in every sense of the word. Both pitchers were magnificent, making big pitches whenever they needed them. Justice got the game's first hit, a single in the second, but he was stranded on second base. Harper and Mack singled in the Twins' second, but Smoltz got Pagliarulo on a groundout.

A single and a walk put two Braves on in the third with one out. But Morris bore down to get Pendleton on a fly to left and Gant on a fielder's choice. A Gladden double was wasted in the Minnesota third. The Braves got one hit in the fourth and two more in the fifth, but each time Morris shut the door when he had to. The veteran was bending, but wouldn't break. By the sixth both pitchers seemed to be getting tougher. Neither team had a hit in the sixth or seventh inning. No seventh game of a World Series had gone scoreless for so long.

In the eighth, the Braves threatened again. Smith led off with a single, followed by a Pendleton double to left center. On Pendleton's hit, Smith apparently lost sight of the ball. Second sacker Knoblauch and shortstop Gagne pulled a decoy and Smith stopped at second for several seconds before continuing on to third. Had he seen the ball hit at the base of the wall and kept running, he surely would have scored.

Morris then got Gant to ground to first, the runners holding. Justice was given an intentional walk to load the bases. With the game possibly on the line, Sid Bream hit a hard grounder to Hrbek, who went to the plate to start a slick 3–6–3 double play. Morris and the Twins had dodged a bullet.

Then in the bottom of the eighth it was the Twins' turn. Pinch hitter Randy Bush singled. After Gladden flied to Gant, Knoblauch singled to right, pinch runner Al Newman racing around to third. At that point, Manager Cox pulled Smoltz in favor of lefty Mike Stanton. Puckett was then walked intentionally, loading the sacks. The fans roared as big Kent Hrbek came up.

Stanton delivered and Hrbek smacked a liner toward second. Lemke took two steps to his right, grabbed it, and then stepped on second to complete an unassisted double play. Now the Braves had dodged one. The game went into the ninth, still scoreless, the tension mounting with each pitch.

Despite having pitched in his third game of the Series, Morris worked into the ninth and retired the Braves in order. Now the Twins were up and it was sudden death. A run would end it all. Chili Davis opened things up with a single to right. Jerome Brown ran for him. Brian Harper then pushed a bunt toward second and beat it out for a base hit.

With runners on first and second, Alejandro Pena came into the game. The ace reliever did his thing again, inducing Shane Mack to ground into a double play, Brown taking third. After Pagliarulo drew a walk, Pena bore down to fan Paul Sorrento, ending the threat and sending the game into extra innings for the third time in the series.

To the surprise of nearly everyone, Jack Morris was back on the mound for the 10th inning. The ultimate competitor just refused to come out of the game. And he once again made it look easy, retiring the Braves in 1-2-3 fashion. As Morris walked off the mound to the cheers of the Minnesota fans, there was a feeling in the air that something was going to happen.

It started quickly as lead-off man Gladden splintered his bat on a Pena pitch and still managed to muscle a double to left center. Knoblauch then sacrificed Gladden over to third.

Now the wheels were turning. Manager Cox ordered both Puckett and Hrbek walked intentionally, loading the bases and setting up a potential double play. Manager Kelly countered with the veteran Gene Larkin as a pinch hitter for Brown.

"I went to the plate with two ideas in my head," Larkin said later. "Get a strike and hit it in the air. I knew the fastball was coming, because that's all Pena really throws. I was ready for it."

Sure enough, Pena's first pitch was a fastball and Larkin swung. As soon as he hit it, he thrust his fist into the air and trotted toward first. Gladden, standing on third base, also thrust his fist into the air. Brian Hunter, playing very shallow in left, took two steps back, then stopped. The ball sailed over his head and dropped to the turf. Gladden trotted home with the winning run and pandemonium broke loose. The Twins had won the game and the Series, 1–0. They had done it just the way they had in 1987, winning all four games at the Metrodome.

Morris had been nothing short of brilliant. He threw a 10-inning, 7-hit shutout to win not only his second game of the Series, but the Most Valuable Player prize as well.

"Hindsight is twenty-twenty, but this is why the Twins signed Jack," said teammate Al Newman. "From the first day of the season, he was the guy. He was spectacular."

Morris, of course, was ecstatic. "You just dream about these things," he gushed. "I guess some baseball god in the sky was blessing me."

It was something baseball had dreamed about too, a great World Series that gripped a nation. It was clean, free of any real controversy, well played, and full of tension. In fact, many were calling it the greatest World Series ever.

Former Cincinnati Reds star turned broadcaster Johnny Bench recalled being in a few Series himself. "It's hard when you play in one yourself to say this one was better," said Bench, "because you lived through the gut-wrenching moments and you never forget the feeling.

"But I tell you, I can't remember watching a more enjoyable Series than this one. The fans in both cities have been unbelievable, and that created an atmosphere of excitement. It was good baseball, a lot of great pitching and defense, and that made for a lot of suspense."

It was a Series where there really weren't any losers. Even the victorious Twins had only good things to say about the vanquished Braves, repeating the sentiment over and over that the Braves were as much winners as they were. And mark the words of the Braves' Terry Pendleton: "I can't remember a Series where every pitch, every inning, every strike, every out mattered so much," he said. "When I came up in the tenth inning Sunday night I was talking to Brian Harper, and he said, 'Why don't we just quit and call it a tie?' "

Perhaps that was the key to the entire 1991 season. Neither the Twins nor the Braves would quit. They were both last-place teams in 1990, teams almost everyone predicted would be at or near the bottom again in 1991. Not only didn't they quit, but the players in both ballclubs raised the level of their game, then raised it again until baseball history was made.

As Jack Morris so ably put it: "There is such a thing as leading by example and I did the best I could do. In Detroit, the guys I looked up to were the guys who took the bull by the horns and made it happen."

Worst to first. It had never happened before. But the Minnesota Twins and Atlanta Braves took that proverbial bull by the horns and did it. From Jack Morris and John Smoltz to the last guy on the bench, they played each game all year as if their lives depended on it. There was no quitting, right until the final out that made the Twins champions. As for the Braves, they might be the runners-up, but they weren't losers. In the eyes of the baseball world, they were champions too.

Atlanta Braves Final Season Statistics

Batting	BA	SLG	OB	G	AB	R	H	TB	2B	3B	HR	RBI	BB	SO	SB	CS	E
Heep	.417	.500	.462	14	12	4	5	6	1	0	0	3	1	4	0	1	0
Treadway	.320	.418	.368	106	306	41	98	128	17	2	3	32	23	19	2	2	15
Pendleton	.319	.517	.363	153	586	94	187	303	34	8	22	86	43	70	10	2	24
Mitchell	.318	.409	.392	48	66	11	21	27	0	0	2	5	8	12	3	1	1
Nixon	.297	.327	.371	124	401	81	119	131	10	1	0	26	47	40	72	21	3
Justice	.275	.503	.377	109	396	67	109	199	25	1	21	87	65	81	8	8	7
L. Smith	.275	.394	.377	122	353	58	97	139	19	1	7	44	50	64	9	5	5
Blauser	.259	.409	.358	129	352	49	91	144	14	3	11	54	25	59	5	6	17
Bream	.253	.423	.313	91	265	32	67	112	12	0	11	45	25	31	0	3	3
Gant	.251	.496	.338	154	561	101	141	278	35	3	32	105	71	104	34	15	6
Hunter	.251	.450	.296	97	271	32	68	122	16	1	12	50	17	48	0	2	8
Belliard	.249	.286	.296	149	353	36	88	101	9	2	0	27	22	63	3	1	18
Cabrera	.242	.432	.284	44	95	7	23	41	6	0	6	23	6	20	1	1	3
Olson	.241	.345	.316	133	411	46	99	142	25	0	6	44	44	48	1	1	4
Lemke	.234	.312	.305	136	269	36	63	84	11	2	2	23	29	27	1	2	10
Willard	.214	.429	.313	17	14	1	3	6	0	0	1	4	2	5	0	0	0
Heath	.209	.266	.250	49	139	4	29	37	3	1	1	12	7	26	0	0	2
Castilla	.200	.200	.200	12	5	1	1	1	0	0	0	0	0	2	0	0	0
Sanders	.191	.345	.270	54	110	16	21	38	1	2	4	13	12	23	11	3	3
Berryhill	.188	.325	.243	63	160	13	30	52	7	0	5	14	11	42	1	2	8
Gregg	.187	.308	.275	72	107	13	20	33	8	1	1	4	12	24	2	2	0
Bell	.133	.233	.188	17	30	4	4	7	0	0	1	1	2	7	1	0	2
Rossy	.000	.000	.000	5	1	0	0	0	0	0	0	0	0	1	0	0	0

Pitching	W-L	ERA	G	GS	CG	GF	ShO	SV	IP	H	R	ER	HR	BB	SO
Berenguer	0-3	2.24	49	0	0	35	0	17	64.1	43	18	16	5	20	53
Pena	8-1	2.40	59	0	0	36	0	15	82.1	74	23	22	6	22	62
Glavine	20-11	2.55	34	34	9	0	1	0	246.2	201	83	70	17	69	192
Mercker	5-3	2.58	50	4	0	28	0	6	73.1	56	23	21	5	35	62
Stanton	5-5	2.88	74	0	0	20	0	7	78	62	27	25	6	21	54
Freeman	1-0	3.00	34	0	0	6	0	1	48	37	19	16	2	13	34
Wohlers	3-1	3.20	17	0	0	4	0	2	19.2	17	7	7	1	13	13
Avery	18-8	3.38	35	35	3	0	1	0	210.1	189	89	79	21	65	137
Leibrandt	15-13	3.49	36	36	1	0	1	0	229.2	212	105	89	18	56	128
Smoltz	14-13	3.80	36	36	5	0	0	0	229.2	206	101	97	16	77	148
Clancy	3-5	3.91	54	0	0	22	0	8	89.2	73	42	39	8	34	50
St. Claire	0-0	4.08	19	0	0	5	0	0	28.2	31	17	13	4	9	30
Bielecki	13-11	4.46	41	25	0	9	0	0	173.2	171	91	86	18	56	75
Mahler	2-4	4.50	23	8	0	2	0	0	66	70	37	33	4	28	27
Sisk	2-1	5.02	14	0	0	2	0	0	14.1	21	14	8	1	8	5
P. Smith	1-3	5.06	14	10	0	2	0	0	48	48	33	27	5	22	29
Petry	0-0	5.55	10	0	0	4	0	0	24.1	29	17	15	2	14	9
Reynoso	2-1	6.17	6	5	0	1	0	0	23.1	26	18	16	4	10	10
Parrett	1-2	6.33	18	0	0	9	0	1	21.1	31	18	15	2	12	14

Minnesota Twins Final Season Statistics

Batting	BA	SLG	OB	G	AB	R	H	TB	2B	3B	HR	RBI	BB	SO	SB	CS	E
Puckett	.319	.460	.352	152	611	92	195	281	29	6	15	89	31	78	11	5	6
Harper	.311	.447	.336	123	441	54	137	197	28	1	10	69	14	22	1	2	8
Mack	.310	.529	.363	143	442	79	137	234	27	8	18	74	34	79	13	9	7
Bush	.303	.485	.401	93	165	21	50	80	10	1	6	23	24	25	0	2	2
Webster	.294	.588	.390	18	34	7	10	20	1	0	3	8	6	10	0	0	1
Leius	.286	.417	.378	109	199	35	57	83	7	2	5	20	30	35	5	5	7
Larkin	.286	.373	.361	98	255	34	73	95	14	1	2	19	30	21	2	3	3
Hrbek	.284	.461	.373	132	462	72	131	213	20	1	20	89	67	48	5	4	8
Munoz	.283	.500	.327	51	138	15	39	69	7	1	7	26	9	31	4	0	8
Knoblauch	.281	.350	.351	151	565	78	159	198	24	6	1	50	59	40	25	5	18
Pagliarulo	.279	.384	.322	121	365	38	102	140	20	0	6	36	21	55	1	2	11
Davis	.277	.507	.385	153	534	84	148	271	34	1	29	93	95	117	5	6	0
Gagne	.265	.395	.310	139	408	52	108	161	23	3	8	42	26	72	11	9	9
Sorrento	.255	.553	.314	26	47	6	12	26	2	0	4	13	4	11	0	0	0
Gladden	.247	.356	.306	126	461	65	114	164	14	9	6	52	36	60	15	9	3
Brown	.216	.216	.256	38	37	10	8	8	0	0	0	0	2	8	7	1	1
Ortiz	.209	.261	.293	61	134	9	28	35	5	1	0	11	15	12	0	1	1
Newman	.191	.211	.260	118	246	25	47	52	5	0	0	19	23	21	4	5	4
Castillo	.167	.333	.231	9	12	0	2	4	0	1	0	0	0	2	0	0	0

Pitching	W-L	ERA	G	GS	CG	GF	ShO	SV	IP	H	R	ER	HR	BB	SO
Aguilera	4–5	2.35	63	0	0	60	0	42	69	44	20	18	3	30	61
Willis	8–3	2.63	40	0	0	9	0	2	89	76	31	26	4	19	35
Tapani	16–9	2.99	34	34	4	0	1	0	244	225	84	81	23	40	135
Erickson	20–8	3.18	32	32	5	0	3	0	204	189	80	72	13	71	108
Morris	18–12	3.43	35	35	10	0	2	0	246.2	226	107	94	18	92	163
Leach	1–2	3.61	50	0	0	22	0	0	67.1	82	28	27	3	14	32
Neagle	0–1	4.05	7	3	0	2	0	0	20	28	9	9	3	7	14
Edens	2–2	4.09	8	6	0	0	0	0	33	34	15	15	2	10	19
Guthrie	7–5	4.32	41	12	0	13	0	2	98	116	52	47	11	41	72
Bedrosian	5–3	4.42	56	0	0	22	0	6	77.1	70	42	38	11	35	44
West	4–4	4.54	15	12	0	0	0	0	71.1	66	37	36	13	28	52
Abbott	3–1	4.75	15	3	0	1	0	0	47.1	38	27	25	5	36	43
Anderson	5–11	4.96	29	22	2	4	0	0	134.1	148	82	74	24	42	51
Wayne	1–0	5.11	8	0	0	2	0	1	12.1	11	7	7	1	4	7
Banks	1–1	5.71	5	3	0	2	0	0	17.1	21	15	11	1	12	16
Casian	0–0	7.36	15	0	0	4	0	0	18.1	28	16	15	4	7	6

Atlanta Braves Final World Series Statistics

Batting	G	AB	R	H	2B	3B	HR	RBI	SO	BB	Avg.
Lemke	6	24	4	10	1	3	0	4	4	2	.417
Belliard	7	16	0	6	1	0	0	4	2	1	.375
Pendleton	7	30	6	11	3	0	2	3	1	3	.367
Gant	7	30	3	8	0	1	0	4	3	2	.267
Justice	7	27	5	7	0	0	2	6	5	5	.259
Treadway	3	4	1	1	0	0	0	0	2	1	.250
Smith	7	26	5	6	0	0	3	3	4	3	.231
Olson	7	27	3	6	2	0	0	1	4	5	.222
Hunter	7	21	2	4	1	0	1	3	2	0	.190
Blauser	5	6	0	1	0	0	0	0	1	1	.167
Bream	7	24	0	3	2	0	0	0	4	3	.125
Cabrera	3	1	0	0	0	0	0	0	0	0	.000
Clancy	2	1	0	0	0	0	0	0	1	0	.000
Glavine	2	2	0	0	0	0	0	0	0	0	.000
Mitchell	3	2	0	0	0	0	0	0	1	0	.000
Smoltz	2	2	0	0	0	0	0	0	1	0	.000
Avery	2	3	0	0	0	0	0	0	2	0	.000
Gregg	4	3	0	0	0	0	0	0	2	0	.000
Leibrandt	2	0	0	0	0	0	0	0	0	0	—
Mercker	2	0	0	0	0	0	0	0	0	0	—
Pena	3	0	0	0	0	0	0	0	0	0	—
St. Claire	1	0	0	0	0	0	0	0	0	0	—

Batting (Cont.)	G	AB	R	H	2B	3B	HR	RBI	SO	BB	Avg.
Stanton	5	0	0	0	0	0	0	0	0	0	—
Willard	1	0	0	0	0	0	0	1	0	0	—
Wohlers	3	0	0	0	0	0	0	0	0	0	—
Totals	7	249	29	63	10	4	8	29	39	26	.253

Pitching	G	CG	IP	H	R	BB	SO	HB	WP	W	L	Sv	ERA
Stanton	5	0	7.1	5	0	2	7	0	0	1	0	0	0.00
Wohlers	3	0	1.2	2	0	2	1	0	0	0	0	0	0.00
Mercker	2	0	1	0	0	0	1	0	0	0	0	0	0.00
Smoltz	2	0	14.1	13	2	1	11	1	0	0	1	0	1.26
Glavine	2	1	13.1	8	6	7	8	0	0	1	1	0	2.70
Pena	3	0	5.1	6	2	3	7	0	1	0	0	0	3.38
Avery	2	0	13	10	6	1	8	0	0	0	0	0	3.46
Clancy	3	0	4.1	3	2	4	2	0	0	1	0	0	4.15
St. Claire	1	0	1	1	1	0	0	0	0	0	0	0	9.00
Leibrandt	2	0	4	8	5	1	3	0	0	0	2	0	11.25
Totals	7	1	65.1	56	24	21	48	1	1	3	4	0	2.89

Minnesota Twins Final World Series Statistics

Batting	G	AB	R	H	2B	3B	HR	RBI	SO	BB	Avg.
Larkin	4	4	0	2	0	0	0	1	0	0	.500
Newman	3	2	0	1	0	1	0	1	0	0	.500
Harper	7	21	2	8	2	0	0	1	2	2	.381
Leius	7	14	2	5	0	0	1	2	2	1	.357
Knoblauch	7	26	3	8	1	0	0	2	2	4	.308
Pagliarulo	6	11	1	3	0	0	1	2	2	1	.273
Puckett	7	24	4	6	0	1	2	4	7	5	.250
Bush	3	4	0	1	0	0	0	0	1	0	.250
Gladden	7	30	5	7	2	2	0	0	4	3	.233
Davis	6	18	4	4	0	0	2	4	3	2	.222
Ortiz	3	5	0	1	0	0	0	1	1	0	.200
Gagne	7	24	1	4	1	0	1	3	7	0	.167
Mack	6	23	0	3	1	0	0	1	7	0	.130
Hrbek	7	26	2	3	1	0	1	2	6	2	.115
Aguilera	4	1	0	0	0	0	0	0	0	0	.000
Erickson	2	1	0	0	0	0	0	0	1	0	.000
Tapani	1	1	0	0	0	0	0	0	0	0	.000
Brown	4	2	0	0	0	0	0	0	0	0	.000
Morris	3	2	0	0	0	0	0	0	1	0	.000
Sorrento	3	2	0	0	0	0	0	0	2	1	.000
Bedrosian	3	0	0	0	0	0	0	0	0	0	.000
Guthrie	4	0	0	0	0	0	0	0	0	0	—

Batting (Cont.)	G	AB	R	H	2B	3B	HR	RBI	SO	BB	Avg.
Leach	2	0	0	0	0	0	0	0	0	0	—
West	1	0	0	0	0	0	0	0	0	0	—
Willis	4	0	0	0	0	0	0	0	0	0	—
Totals	7	241	24	56	8	4	8	24	48	21	.232

Pitching	G	CG	IP	H	R	BB	SO	HB	WP	W	L	Sv	ERA
Morris	3	1	23	18	3	9	15	0	2	2	0	0	1.17
Aguilera	4	0	5	6	1	1	3	0	0	1	1	2	1.80
Guthrie	4	0	4	3	1	4	3	0	1	0	1	0	2.25
Leach	2	0	2.1	2	1	0	2	0	0	0	0	0	3.86
Tapani	2	0	12	13	6	2	7	0	0	1	1	0	4.50
Erickson	2	0	10.2	10	7	4	5	1	1	0	0	0	5.06
Willis	4	0	7	6	4	2	2	0	0	0	0	0	5.14
Bedrosian	3	0	3.1	3	2	0	2	0	1	0	0	0	5.40
West	2	0	0	2	4	4	0	0	0	0	0	0	—
Totals	7	0	67.1	63	29	26	39	1	5	4	3	2	3.74